Labor, Economy, and Society

Economy and Society

Labor, Economy, and Society

Jeffrey J. Sallaz

polity

First published in 2013 by Polity Press

Polity Press
65 Bridge Street
Cambridge CB2 1UR, UK

Polity Press
350 Main Street
Malden, MA 02148, USA

ISBN-13: 978-0-7456-5366-2
ISBN-13: 978-0-7456-5367-9(pb)

A catalogue record for this book is available from the British Library.

Typeset in 11 on 13 pt Sabon
by Servis Filmsetting Ltd, Stockport, Cheshire
Printed and bound in Great Britain by the MPG Books Group

For further information on Polity, visit our website: www.politybooks.com

Contents

List of Figures

1

Introduction: What Good is Work?

[I]f the concept of labor – which in its hitherto accepted generality has given a vague feeling rather than a definite content to its meaning – is to acquire such a definite meaning, then it requires that a greater precision be given to the real process which one understands as labor. (Simmel 2011 [1907]: 453)

It often seems as though capitalist societies exist in a state of perpetual crisis regarding the issue of work. Consider the United States, long home to the world's largest economy and where, in 2008, a financial crisis originating in the housing sector triggered a severe and extended economic slow-down. As the "Great Recession" entrenched itself, indebted consumers cut back on spending while businesses and governments scaled back hiring and laid off employees. By 2011 the country as a whole was 12 million jobs short of the number needed to provide employment for all eligible adults – not to mention the additional 25 million people working part-time but desiring full-time work.

The nation's mood was dark, to say the least. Night after night, news programs featured heartbreaking stories of hopeless job-seekers queuing up at employment agencies. Politicians from both sides of the aisle hammered Democratic President Barack Obama for his lack of a comprehensive "jobs plan" to address an unemployment rate hovering around 10 percent. While many offered different remedies for what ailed the economy, the underlying diagnosis was widely agreed upon: industrious Americans were desperately seeking work, but the jobs were simply not there.

In the midst of such a crisis, it was only too easy to forget that scarcely a decade before – in fact, during the previous Democratic presidential administration – the United States faced the opposite problem. During the 1990s, driven by a dot-com investment boom, stock markets increased in value, consumers went on a spending binge, and firms went on a hiring spree. With the unemployment rate dropping under 4 percent and a surplus of job openings, the American economy was plagued not by a lack of jobs but by a lack of workers! Especially for employers in the low-wage sectors of the economy (such as food service and home health care), it was difficult to attract staff at the prevailing minimum wage. The dominant discourse on employment shifted as well, and it soon became bipartisan "common sense" that the problem haunting America was an eroding work ethic.

The system of entitlements that had been put in place over the preceding decades to protect vulnerable Americans, this thinking went, had backfired. An overly generous "welfare state" had created a coddled and indolent class of job-shirkers (Collins and Mayer 2010). In truth, even at its peak, the welfare system in the Unites States was less generous than that of other rich industrialized nations (Esping-Andersen 1990; Steensland 2007). Nonetheless, President Clinton, in 1996, signed the Personal Responsibility and Work Opportunity Act, a piece of legislation intended to "end welfare as we know it" (Clinton 2006). It forced recipients of public assistance to sing for their proverbial suppers, no matter how menial the employment they acquired.

A seemingly permanent "crisis of work" is not unique to the United States. For some time now, Europe has been plagued by high unemployment and economic stagnation, a situation many attribute to inflexible labor markets. Burdensome state regulations and powerful labor unions, critics argue, have made it difficult for firms to hire and fire workers in response to fast-shifting business conditions.

Meanwhile, in China, decades of economic reform have liberalized the economy and produced staggering economic growth. In

Introduction: What Good is Work?

Introduction: What Good is Work?

fact, in early 2011, China surpassed Japan to become the world's second largest economy. Accompanying this rise in output, however, has been a surge in protests and strikes by workers in the country's burgeoning factory system (Lee 2007). As they produce more and more goods for the world's (and especially America's) consumers, Chinese workers appear to be increasingly unsatisfied with their poor working conditions and lack of socio-economic mobility. Similar stories of labor discontent can be found in the world's other emerging economies, such as Brazil, South Korea, South Africa, and India (Silver 2003).

The purpose of this book is to mobilize the conceptual tools of economic sociology to understand the place and fate of work under global capitalism. Economic sociology is ideally suited to this task. As an academic field it endeavors to put capitalism in world-historical perspective, as but one among many potential ways to organize economic activity. How, it asks, did private property and labor markets come to constitute the pillars of the modern global order? Why is the contemporary world converging upon an extreme version of capitalism (the free-market, or neoliberal, version most closely associated with the United States)? Is it folly to even imagine a post-capitalist future?

To address such questions, economic sociologists have assembled a range of theories, ideas, and methods. At the center of and unifying this assemblage is one key insight: that markets are social structures (Martin 2009). They come into being not as the expression of some natural law, but as strategic action projects that achieve success at particular historical moments (Fligstein and McAdam 2012; Hall and Soskice 2001). Markets of labor are no exception. To transform the basic human capacity to engage in meaningful work into a commodity requires persuasion, coercion, and ongoing intervention. To challenge the resulting fiction requires strategic action as well. As the paradigm of regulated capitalism (in which labor is afforded basic protections from the constant pressure of the market) gives way to unfettered market fundamentalism, it becomes ever more important to understand how these conflicts over labor's status as a commodity play out.

3

Of Metaphors and Markets

People have a natural tendency to think metaphorically. When confronted with something new and puzzling, we make sense of it by comparing it to something that is already available in our vocabulary. It is thus not surprising that so many observers look at the crises of work that continue to plague us and attempt to make sense of them through *organic* or *mechanical* metaphors. That is, they compare the society under consideration to a sick person or a malfunctioning machine. If the unemployment rate in France suddenly spikes, we will surely hear a diagnosis of "Eurosclerosis." If the United States' inflation rate is too high, it could well be the case that the country's "jobs machine" is "overheating." And just as a physician prescribes a cure or a mechanic proposes a fix, the observer feels compelled to propose a line of action (typically a new policy or the modification of an existing one) that will bring the economy back to a healthy condition.

But what exactly would such a condition look like? How often, and for how long, do actually existing capitalist economies appear to exist in such a state? Let's return to the example of the United States. Many have argued that it most closely approximates a pure, or, in the words of the sociologist Max Weber, "ideal type" capitalist economy. Among all the countries in the world today, that is, the United States most fully embraces the principles of private property and market exchange. Not only the United States' continued leadership in the world economy, but the fact that so many countries have attempted to imitate its model of economic regulation over the past several decades, suggests that the US system of capitalism, despite its recent weaknesses, will continue to be a dominant paradigm for the foreseeable future. Nonetheless, even a cursory glance confirms that the US economy is notable precisely for its continual failure to meet its own standards of a "healthy" work system (Mishel et al., 2009).

Consider a handful of basic indicators, starting with an unemployment rate that recently peaked at 10 percent. Economists and policy-makers speak of a salubrious state of "full employment." Somewhat counterintuitively, this does not mean a situation in

4

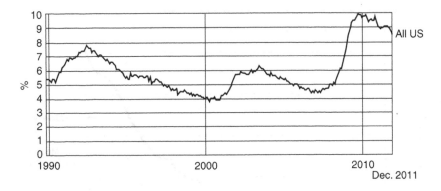

Data source: Bureau of Labor Statistics.

Figure 1.1 US unemployment rate, 1990–2011

which every single person who seeks a job will be able to find one, but rather one in which 95 percent of job-seekers can and do. In other words, an unemployment rate of 5 percent is acknowledged to be ideal for a well-functioning capitalist economy. However, if we look at the data for the past two decades (figure 1.1), we see that the actual unemployment rate hits this number only sporadically, on its way up or down. It's as if a hospital patient's temperature could not be maintained at a steady 98.6 degrees Fahrenheit, but swung back and forth between a bad fever and awful chills!

We can also consider the relationship between American workers' productivity and their wages. Productivity refers to the amount of value that is produced by a worker in a given period of time and with a constant amount of inputs. According to some versions of economic theory (along with common principles of fairness), an increase in a worker's productivity should be matched by an increase in that worker's remuneration. This pattern certainly held for the early and middle parts of the twentieth century (see figure 1.2). However, for the past forty years – since approximately 1970 – the two figures have been decoupled: annual increases in worker productivity have not been rewarded with proportional increases in employee compensation (as inferred from trends in median family income). While American workers

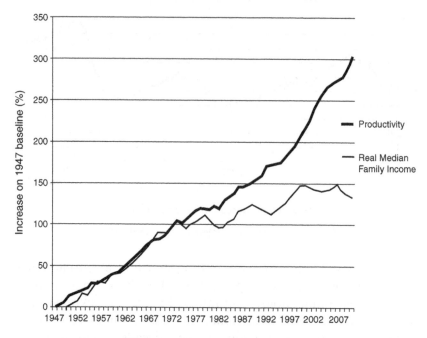

Data source: US Census Bureau and Economic Policy Institute.

Figure 1.2 Productivity growth versus real median family income growth in the United States since 1947

produce much more value today than they did twenty or thirty years ago, the size of their paychecks has budged barely at all. In fact, many have hypothesized that this discrepancy was one of the primary causes of the Great Recession that commenced in 2008: denied raises at work, American households turned *en masse* to credit card debt, reverse mortgages, and other unsound financial instruments to fund their consumption and maintain their standards of living (Reich 2010).

If capitalism is like a patient who is perpetually sick, how are we to explain its global dominance today? Perhaps an organic metaphor is *not* the optimal one after all. Let us consider instead the viewpoints of two early theorists of capitalism whose work remains central to the field of economic sociology: Karl Marx and Joseph Schumpeter.

Both of these thinkers eschewed metaphors depicting capitalism as an organism existing complacently in a state of harmonious equilibrium with its environment. Rather, they conceptualized capitalism as a dynamic, contentious, and continuously evolving *social structure*. For the nineteenth-century German philosopher Marx, this was a revolutionary system that generated immense wealth and unleashed powerful new methods of production. As a byproduct, however, capitalism generated repeated booms and busts, periods of economic expansion and contraction. Eventually, Marx argued, humanity would tire of weathering these repeated crises and, led by an alienated but mobilized working class, institute a post-capitalist, or communist, society characterized by collective ownership of the means of production, rational planning, and an equitable distribution of wealth.

Schumpeter, an Austrian economist of the early twentieth century, concurred with Marx's assessment that capitalism possessed the unique ability to repeatedly revolutionize accepted ways of making and doing things. As the forces of supply and demand ran their course, they would select for those market actors most suited for survival. He labeled this process, in which existing businesses were eviscerated and new ones brought into being, one of creative destruction (Schumpeter 1994 [1942]). And though Schumpeter himself believed that capitalism could not survive these eternally recurring purges, other luminaries of economic thought (e.g., Friedman 2002 [1962]; Hayek 1996 [1948]) argued the converse: although the business cycle could be painful, especially for those industries and trades that became outmoded and were displaced, on the whole a system of private ownership and market competition was the only way that society could evolve and improve. The communist system that Marx proposed, in contrast, would ultimately stifle humanity's entrepreneurial spirit.

In many ways, the story of the twentieth century was one of these contrasting visions. Following the Second World War, there arose a new global order centered upon a conflict between two economic systems: that of the United States – champion of free-market capitalism – and that of the Soviet Union—whose leaders embraced, at least in principle, the central tenets of Marxism. At no point did these conflicting visions erupt into direct military confrontation between the two sides. Rather, there played out a Cold War in which each nation sought to expand its political influence throughout key geographical areas and to exercise cultural hegemony in the emergent "world society." In addition, and perhaps most importantly, the United States and the Soviet Union engaged in frantic contests to design innovative and efficient methods of production. The most high profile of these took place in the fields of aeronautics (the "space race") and weaponry (the "arms race"). But across all sectors of their economies, the two nations implemented divergent methods of organizing work and workers: the one based on central planning and state ownership, the other on market forces and private property (Burawoy and Lukács 1985).

In 1991 the Soviet Union collapsed and the Cold War ended. It is debatable the extent to which the Soviet Union's demise was attributable to inherent failings in a socialist system of production. In some ways it was remarkable that Russia, a rural and feudal society on the eve of its 1917 revolution, was able to transform itself into a global industrial powerhouse over the course of the twentieth century. Regardless, the collapse of the Soviet Union signaled the triumph of Schumpterian-style capitalism. Throughout the 1980s and 1990s, not only the former Soviet states but countries worldwide reformed their economic systems in line with the principle that the free market (and not central planning by state bureaucrats, traditional authorities, or an enlightened proletariat) should guide the production, distribution, and consumption of valued goods, services, and resources (Baccaro and Howell 2011).

In regard to the issue of work, the implications of this neoliberal revolution were clear. To increase productivity, maximize efficiency, and improve competitiveness, policy-makers must *treat human labor like any other resource: that is, as a commodity to be bought and sold on the open market.* British Prime Minister Margaret Thatcher, who, along with US President Ronald Reagan, spearheaded this neoliberal paradigm shift by launching attacks on labor unions and other institutions intended to protect workers from the vagaries of the market, famously stated the new common sense thus: from this day forward, "there is no alternative" to free-market capitalism (Harvey 2007).

But was this final chapter penned too soon? Even prior to the recession that hit in 2008, "crises of work" had not disappeared. If anything, they arose again and again, with what seemed like an ever-increasing frequency. In addition to the issues mentioned above (of unemployment, welfare reform, and stagnant wages), work remains implicated in a good many of the social problems confronting our world today: increasing inequality, illegal immigration, illicit discrimination, and on and on (Sassen 1998). In the words of economist Meghnad Desai (2004), it may be that we are witnessing "Marx's revenge." That is, despite the claims of free-market advocates, a system that treats human labor as a simple commodity is destined for instability. Nonetheless, with the dramatic end of Soviet socialism along with communist China's continued drift toward a market system, there do seem to be few alternatives at hand.

Rather than a resurrection of Marx from the grave, it seems more likely that our era will remain one of "zombie economics" (Quiggin 2010) in which empirically discredited ideas – namely, absolute faith in the beneficence of free markets – continue to guide us. Now more than ever we need new concepts to dissect the *social processes* through which markets are produced and sustained in practice. This is especially true for markets in labor. It was capitalism's greatest feat to transform the human capacity to work into a substance that can be bought and sold; while few other transformations have evoked such a backlash from society. To document how work is sustained as a "fictitious commodity" under capitalism constitutes the central task of what we propose to be a *critical economic sociology of labor*. As with all endeavors, it should commence from first principles.

Labor as Fictitious Commodity

It is a foundational anthropological fact that human societies have to find a way to get things done. At some point in the distant future we may all live like the cartoon Jetsons, with robotic butlers to cater to our every need. But even then, actual humans will be needed to design, distribute, update, and repair them. In short, work will always be with us.

We may give this activity of work a very general definition. It is the *process whereby human beings transform the things of the world to create value*. These "things" may be material, as when a bitter lemon and granular sugar are stirred into delicious lemonade, or they may be immaterial, as when a composer channels an artistic impulse into a haunting melody. They may even be one's own body, as when a professional marathoner trains to improve her racing time. Furthermore, the value that is produced through work may derive from the product's use to the producer, as when that pitcher of lemonade is consumed by the lemonade-maker and his friends for hydration, vitamin C, and pure enjoyment. Or the product of work may be valuable because it can subsequently be exchanged for other things. This would occur if an extra glass from that pitcher of lemonade was sold and the proceeds used to purchase an accompanying pastry.

If the inescapability of work is an anthropological reality, so too is the fact of *tremendous variation in how work is accomplished in different places and at different times*. Once we widen our gaze from the individual producer to the wider society, a series of questions arise. Who controls the raw materials, or inputs, needed to engage in work, and who can claim ownership of the value, or output, that results? Given that the actual doing of work can be unpleasant, tiresome, and dangerous, what sorts of motivations are needed to get people to engage in production? How are different trades distributed and coordinated across society as a whole? (We certainly would not want a world in which everyone made lemonade for a living.)

Throughout history, we observe a wide range of answers to such questions. In slave societies such as ancient Greece or the American South up until the nineteenth century, entire classes of people were dehumanized, forced into bondage, and driven to work for a property-owning class. Then there are communal social systems (typically small in scale) in which all members voluntarily take part in work and equally divide among themselves the value that is thereby produced: examples would include an Israeli kibbutz and a non-profit arts festival (Chen 2009). Between these extremes of coercion and cooperation is found capitalism.

In an ideal-typical capitalist social system, work is organized as marketized employment and legitimated by a series of myths. The first is that modern societies have happened upon the optimal way of organizing production: as a transaction between an employer who supplies the inputs and an employee who creates value from them. Second, the content of the exchange between these two parties can be specified thus: an employee receives financial remuneration in return for her effort. Third, the terms of the exchange (i.e., how much remuneration is provided) are fair. Want to know why your salary is what it is? It's simply a matter of the market for labor in your trade establishing an equilibrium between demand and supply. As a worker, you decide the lowest, or reservation, wage at which you will accept a job, while employers raise their offers until a clearing price is reached. In sum, by allowing the market to guide the myriad exchanges between workers and employers, capitalism stimulates innovation, properly rewards effort, and creates a prosperous society.

Like all gospels, this one has its skeptics. If Marx was the most prominent of the nineteenth century, the title for the twentieth must surely go to the Hungarian social theorist Karl Polanyi (Polanyi-Levitt and Mendell 1987). In his masterpiece, *The Great Transformation* (2001 [1944]: 29), Polanyi excoriated the "utopian endeavor of economic liberalism to set up a self-regulating market system." While small-scale markets had existed throughout human history, it was only with the advent of modern capitalism that three key substances – *land, money, and labor* – were brought into the market system. The problem, however, is that natural resources, symbolic currencies, and human creativities are *not* created to serve as commodities. When you systematically price, buy, and sell them, you distort and ultimately destroy them. For this reason, Polanyi referred to land, money, and labor as *fictitious commodities* whose uprooting from traditional social structures will generate backlash and counter-movements.

Extending Polanyi's original insights, economic sociologists have documented how, precisely, markets are constituted as social structures (Bandelj 2009b; Beckert 2002; Fligstein 1996; Nee 1998; Sutton et al. 1994). The general story is that proponents of economic liberalism seek to extend the logic of the market into new arenas; opponents of this logic push back; and from this dialectic there emerge unique hybrids of economic and non-economic practices. In other words, unlike the textbook model of markets as spaces wherein supply meets demand via self-interested transacting, real-world markets remain *embedded* in a variety of domains collectively dubbed "the social" (Storper and Salais 1997).

Three of these domains in particular deserve attention: the *cultural*, the *collective*, and the *cognitive*. By the cultural, economic sociologists refer to the innate tendency for human groups to imbue economic phenomena (such as acts of production and exchange) with meaning via rich symbolic systems. Moral obligations, collective narratives, and aesthetic principles are just some of the cultural process that can be said to ground markets in the social. By collective embeddedness we refer to the social structures in which market participants are located and which shape their behavior in ways that cannot be described by methodological individualism. Examples here range from political fields to interpersonal networks to small-group situations. Finally, the notion of cognitive embeddedness captures how and why behavior departs from the predictions of doctrinaire rational choice theories. Biographical experience, decision-making heuristics, and even one's religious faith have all been shown to influence the choices made in markets.

Equipped with this theoretical toolkit, economic sociologists have documented the social structuring of a wide variety of markets: dollars and pesos, kidneys and cotton, rain forests and fire insurance, sperm and eggs, and on and on. Relatively neglected within this research program, however, has been the question of how markets in human labor are sustained. This is curious insofar as labor was one of the original members of Polanyi's triad of fictitious commodities. Why did labor disappear from the research agenda? It's hard to say exactly, but the effect has been to cede the subject to labor process scholars, industrial psychologists, human resources specialists, behavioral economists, inequality specialists, and organization ethnographers. What is lacking, and what this volume provides, is a single source that ties together key theoretical insights of economic sociology with the impressive empirical studies produced by these latter literatures.

Overview of the Argument

The structure of the argument differs from that of a standard sociology textbook. The latter is typically organized according to the themes that dominate public discourse on employment and its problems. And so we find chapters on unemployment, job satisfaction, management styles, the service sector, strike activity, and so on. While all of these topics will be addressed in the pages to follow, the chapters themselves derive from our central thesis: that *markets for labor, the penultimate fictitious commodity, are social structures.* Indeed, an implicit goal of this book is to encourage readers to think critically about the accepted, "common-sense" categories through which work is commonly discussed and evaluated.

The initial two chapters provide a primer on *the historical and cultural foundations* of commodified labor. Chapter 2, "The Great Transformation of Work," discusses how formal employment came to supplant other ways of creating value as the normative form of work during the eighteenth and nineteenth centuries. Rejecting the technological determinism that underlies standard accounts of an "industrial revolution," it emphasizes how advances in technology, machinery, and industry were part and parcel of larger shifts in governance, organization, and culture. It also summarizes the work of several classical theorists notable for how they situated everyday practices of work in relation to these macro-shifts. These include Adam Smith, a philosopher of the Scottish Enlightenment who elaborated an intellectual and moral justification for market society; Marx, who believed that the exploitation underlying marketized labor would eventually drive workers to overthrow capitalism; early sociologists such as Max Weber, Georg Simmel, and Émile Durkheim, all of whom believed that capitalism could overcome its various pathologies; and Polanyi, who argued that free markets in labor are a fiction requiring constant management lest they spontaneously combust.

Chapter 3, "Classifying Labor," argues that capitalism depends upon the stabilization of market employment as a valid cultural category. The stay-at-home parent, the drug dealer, and the volunteer all transform the world in a way that can be said to add value to it. They all work. But capitalism recognizes as legitimate *only* employment in the labor market for a wage. That this narrow vision of work is not natural in the order of things can be surmised from the unending disputes within capitalist societies over who precisely counts as a worker. Much is at stake in these boundary disputes. If your labor is classified as employment, you achieve certain rights (such as the ability to unionize) but also certain responsibilities (such as the obligation to pay taxes on your earnings). Ultimately, it is the state that possesses the authority to validate such classifications, raising the issue of how cultural meanings, economic interests, and governance regimes intersect.

The next two chapters elucidate the social mechanisms necessary to *accomplish wage labor in practice.* Chapter 4, "Commensurating Labor," asks of employment a question relevant to all types of exchange: how is an equivalency established between substance A and substance B? Under capitalism, an employer and an employee (as well as the institutions that regulate the employment relationship) must come to an (often tacit) agreement as to what exactly is being exchanged when the former hires the latter. A simple equation such as *wage* = *labor* belies the tremendous variation that research has shown to exist across and within societies as to how the employment exchange is conceptualized. In addition, once labor becomes a commodity, it must be priced. Determining the worth of this particular commodity, however, is not a simple matter of letting the magic of the market do its work. In practice, cultural standards come into play, as illustrated by such issues as minimum versus living wages, and free-trade versus fair-trade principles.

Chapter 5, "Making Labor Markets," broadens our scope beyond the employer–employee dyad. It interprets through an economic sociological lens a vibrant stream of research documenting the mechanisms through which firms find workers, and vice versa. There can be little doubt that real-world labor markets scarcely resemble those supposed by economic models. Every time an elected official caves into xenophobic sentiment by restricting the inflow of skilled immigrants, a manager turns down a qualified job applicant because of the color of her skin, or a job-seeker secures employment through the referral of a distant uncle, we witness the social structuring of the labor market. In addition, labor markets are excellent sites to examine contestations over commodified labor. States, unions, social movements, and others all debate the relative merits of market-based versus traditional mechanisms of employer–employee matching.

The remainder of the book puts front and center the issue of *contested commodification*. Chapter 6, "Controlling Labor," critically interrogates the assumption that wage labor is a consensual exchange between coequals. For various reasons, employees may resist attempts to extract from them a certain amount or type of work at a certain price. For the employer, this introduces the problem of management: that is, of monitoring and controlling the exchange. Many assume this is a simple matter of providing the proper mix of incentives and disincentives. In reality, however, employers in capitalist economies regularly use non-market mechanisms to extract work from employees. This chapter summarizes three such strategies: a reliance upon gift exchange rather than monetary payment to induce effort; the recruitment of workers whose early socialization predisposes them to perform a certain sort of labor; and the structuring of work processes as engrossing games the mastery of which legitimizes labor's commodification.

Chapter 7, "Labor and Group-Making," challenges the assumption that a capitalist labor market is an aggregate of myriad exchanges between individual buyers and sellers of labor. Quite often, both parties to the exchange act collectively rather than individually. The resulting collectivities can exhibit varying degrees of formalization. On the employer side they can range from implicit

15

(and often illicit) understandings to established business associations, and on the employee side they can extend from informal work groups to trade union federations. In this chapter we examine the various bases of power that can facilitate or inhibit collective action in the employment market context.

A concluding chapter, "What Good is Embeddeness?," ponders the future of labor under capitalism. The notion of embeddedness, we argue, proved quite useful for analyzing how labor was socially structured under systems of regulated capitalism. However, the terrain has shifted. Financialization, globalization, and digitization have drastically increased the relative bargaining power of employers vis-à-vis labor. At the same time, governments have opted to withdraw social supports for citizens and protections for workers. In addition to documenting this disembedding of labor, a critical economic sociology should seek to theorize the conditions under which labor can be reembedded in the social.

2

The Great Transformation of Work

Work – the creation of value through the application of effort – has always been with us. But employment has not. Throughout most of recorded history, humans have produced the things they need and want *outside of* the context of wage work in a labor market. A capitalist world of work in fact has relatively recent origins. These are to be found in a series of developments that took place in Europe during the eighteenth and nineteenth centuries, and which soon spread to encompass the entire globe. The common label for this process, which is that of an "industrial revolution," too narrowly focuses upon its technical and economic dimensions. Following Karl Polanyi (2001 [1944]), we understand the current system of global capitalism as the product of a "great transformation" that revolutionized not only industry, but also political, organizational, and cultural life (Smelser 1959).

The purpose of this chapter is not to provide a comprehensive history of this transformation.[1] Rather, it is to lay the foundation for an economic-sociological critique of the assumption, dominant in the world today, that work is synonymous with the market exchange of labor. To do so, we reconstruct a debate among four theoretical traditions (the Smithian, Marxist, sociological, and Polanyian) concerning three key aspects of the great transformation (its origins, consequences, and future). Rather than relics of a distant past, these theories remain salient for understanding current controversies concerning the relative roles that states versus markets should play in regulating work, employers, and labor markets.

The World That Was

The phrase *great transformation* refers to a series of interlinked developments that cumulatively reconfigured everyday life for most Europeans and North Americans over the course of the eighteenth and nineteenth centuries.[2] Primary among these was *industrialization*, a switch in what society makes and how it makes it, with the bulk of production shifting from farming and small-scale crafts to the mass manufacture of goods in factories. Industrialization itself entails *mechanization*, the use of machinery rather than human hands and simple tools to make things, and a *division of labor*, as production processes are broken down into discrete tasks that are then distributed among multiple workers. *Proletarianization* refers to the process whereby the mass of people are rendered incapable of independently producing their basic life necessities, leading to *urbanization* as rural dwellers leave the countryside and head to cities to find employment. The cases of China, south Asia, Latin America, and other industrializing regions of the twentieth and early twenty-first centuries illustrate parallel great transformations: societies reconfigured to accommodate the demands of a capitalist system of marketized wage labor (Arrighi 2009; Wallerstein 2011).

When thinking about the forces driving the great transformation, it is tempting to adopt a narrative grounded in individual genius and technological determinism. Popular culture and school textbooks are in fact replete with tales of great men and their "inventions that changed the world" (Maule 2008). James Watt perfected the steam engine, which powered the cotton mills of Lancashire and turned Britain into the "workshop of the world"; Henry Ford's Model-T laid the groundwork for a system of mass production that made America a global superpower; while, more recently, we find Microsoft's Bill Gates or Facebook's Mark Zuckerburg heralded as entrepreneurs who ushered in an information technology (IT) revolution. The story, in every case, is that of the invention of a new technology (be it a spinning jenny, an automobile, or an operating system) that was technically superior to whatever came before. Workers were recruited to build these new goods, consumers rushed to purchase them, market forces did their work, and the rest, as they say, is history.

Economic sociologists tell a different story about the rise of a modern market economy, one that emphasizes the "noneconomic" dimensions of this development. For instance, many have argued that governments played a fundamental role in facilitating and enabling industrialization (Baron et al. 1986). It will only make sense for business-owners to engage in mass production if they are assured of a reliable supply of raw materials and markets for their finished goods. Prior to the eighteenth century, these conditions were rarely found (Allen 2011). Rather than encouraging domestic production for international trade, the feudal aristocracies and monarchies that had controlled Europe since medieval times monopolized wealth for themselves (in the form of tributes, for example) and imposed stiff tariffs on goods from abroad (a basic principle of mercantilism). In what Marx referred to as a "bourgeois revolution," these old regimes were eclipsed by new political movements representing merchants and other advocates of open markets and free exchange.

This new order developed a philosophy of governance that we take for granted today but which was unheard of at the time: that there exists between citizens and their government a social contract whereby the former consent to be governed by the latter (Rousseau 2009 [1762]). In return, the government provides a broad infrastructure through which individuals are guaranteed "life, liberty, and the pursuit of happiness." As Douglass North (1990) argued, political liberalism entailed the development of concrete institutions for managing the economy and facilitating trade. These included legal guarantees of property rights (Campbell and Lindberg 1990), mechanisms for enforcing contracts between private parties (Carruthers and Ariovich 2004), systems to prevent the depletion of common-pool resources

(Ostrom 1990), as well as laws forbidding the formation of monopolies and trusts (Fligstein 1993).

Another argument made by economic sociologists is that the great transformation was driven by innovations in institutional and organizational design as much as by new machines or technologies (Bendix 1956; North and Thomas 1976). Consider the joint stock company. To start and scale up a mass manufacturing facility for the global market, one usually needs access to sums of money much greater than any one individual's personal holdings (Perrow 2005). By selling small ownership stakes to a great many persons in the form of stock, early entrepreneurs were able to accumulate adequate initial capital to build their factories and mills (and limit their own subsequent liability in the case of business failure). To run these enterprises in turn required new systems of internal administration. At sites like the Ford company's River Rouge factory complex in Michigan (employing 100,000 workers and stretching out over 15 million square feet), it would have been impossible for a single proprietor to personally oversee all stages of production and keep track of the complex web of information and resources that flowed through the plant daily (Cutler 2004). In response, firms increasingly adopted a bureaucratic organization (Crozier 1964).

Though bureaucracies are today often ridiculed as stodgy and inflexible, the sociologist Max Weber argued that they are in fact the most efficient way to organize production for mass markets (Weber 1978 [1922]; see also Swedberg 2000). They allow those who own the enterprise to set broad benchmarks and then delegate responsibility for daily operations to lower-level officials (who ideally are selected because of their training and qualifications). Thus, as much as the spinning jenny or the steam engine, stock markets and bureaucratic administration were responsible for the rise of market society. Resolving subsequent conflict of interests between those who own and those who manage the enterprise has been a constant dilemma for capitalist societies (Chandler 1984; Roe 1996), and one that goes a long way toward explaining ongoing international variation in capitalism (Biggart and Guillén 1999; Dore 1973; Hamilton and Biggart 1988).

Closely related to innovations in governance and organization was a transformation of culture. As a concept, "culture" is notoriously hard to pin down (Swidler 1986). For our purposes, we refer to it as a broadly shared system of meanings, norms, values, and sentiments – culture is the story a society tells itself about itself. Prior to the great transformation, European society understood itself through reference to a feudal code based on religion, honor, and dutiful adherence to custom (Bloch 1964). The emergent market order, in contrast, exalted calculation, individuality, and self-interest. Capitalism, in this formulation, required a moral justification, and, as argued by the economic historian Albert Hirschman (1997 [1977]), it received one through the writings of thinkers such as John Millar, Montesquieu, and especially Adam Smith (whose work we will examine closely in the following section). Self-interest, in this new cultural understanding, was a way to counteract the unruly and destructive influence of our irrational passions. In short, strong voices emerged framing the market as neither immoral nor amoral, but rather as a profoundly beneficent and even moral phenomenon (Fourcade and Healy 2007). But of course not everyone was optimistic about the new market society. For every celebrant there was a critic, for every new business a union organizer, and for every employer association a social movement such as the Luddites: craftsmen who surreptitiously slipped into factories at night and smashed to bits the machines that had replaced them.

There can be no dispute that the emergent world of marketized work was a contentious space. We will devote the remainder of this chapter to reconstructing a debate among several grand theoretical traditions of the eighteenth, nineteenth, and twentieth centuries. Each of these theories sought to place the great transformation within a world-historical perspective. Each understood work – that is, the mundane tasks through which individuals create value and sustain themselves – to be central to this transformation. And each theory remains relevant today. Indeed, many of the arguments about work that play out daily in the halls of parliaments, at academic conferences, on internet blogs, and in everyday shoptalk are but rehashings of these classic theoretical conversations.

For an opening salvo we give the floor to the Scottish philosopher Adam Smith (1723–90). His masterpiece, *The Wealth of Nations* (1904 [1776]), challenged longstanding beliefs about free trade and the division of labor. For Smith, what makes us human is our propensity to trade things, including our own capacity to work. This basic proposition paved a foundation for much of modern economic theory, including the writings of such twentieth-century proponents of liberalism as Joseph Schumpeter, Friedrich Hayek, and Milton Friedman. In fact, insofar as mainstream economic discourse about work and labor is today considered common sense (Block 1990), it would be no exaggeration to say that we live in a Smithian world.

But there are other voices in the debate. One is that of Karl Marx, the German-born philosopher, journalist, and activist who, along with his friend Friedrich Engels, developed a grand-theoretical critique of the new market society. Writing from "ground zero" of the industrial revolution (the urban slums of late eighteenth-century London), Marx somewhat surprisingly praised capitalism for its revolutionary advances in productivity, technology, and invention. However, he believed that capitalism would eventually be superseded by an even better system, which he called communism. Even with the collapse of the Soviet Union and contemporary China's gradual drift away from the principles of communism, the critical Marxist tradition remains relevant today for understanding how work is organized under capitalism.

A related but distinct challenge to the Smithian paradigm came from the new field of sociology. Owing to the efforts of Auguste Comte and Émile Durkheim in France, along with Max Weber and Georg Simmel in Germany, sociology was established and legitimated as an academic discipline during the late nineteenth and early twentieth centuries. Like Marxism, sociology disputed the Smithian notion that the market exchange of human labor was a natural and indisputably good phenomenon. But whereas Marx grounded his analysis in the principle of materialism (the idea that the way in which humans work to satisfy their basic physical needs directly determines the totality of their existence), early sociologists did not completely agree. They argued that social life possesses a *sui generis* character, meaning that such uniquely human institutions as language, religion, and government have a life all their own and can even influence the more basic processes of economic life, including work.

This interplay between the material and the social was of utmost concern to the final participant in our conservation, Karl Polanyi (1886–1964). In writings such as *The Great Transformation* (2001 [1944]), the Hungarian-born philosopher challenged the orthodox economic view that human labor could be treated as a simple commodity. Combining rigorous historical research with a keen political sensibility, Polanyi predicted that the nineteenth-century project to "disembed" markets from their social context would ultimately fail (though for different reasons than those proposed by Marx). Overall, the Polanyian paradigm has had great influence not only in sociology, but also in cultural anthropology, political science, and institutional economics.

We will ask of the above theories three questions. Where do markets for labor come from? What, if anything, is wrong with allowing market forces to structure work? And what does the future hold for work under capitalism?

Birth of a Notion

"Go out there and sell yourself." How many job-seekers have been offered this seemingly timeless piece of advice? Indeed, in a capitalist economy, few notions are more entrenched in our common sense than the idea that upon finishing school, one should seek to sell one's services to an employer. And at the highest possible price (i.e., salary)! To the extent that we accept such notions, we are putting into practice one of the fundamental precepts of Adam Smith. As he traveled around Britain and continental Europe in the late eighteenth century, Smith saw a landscape increasingly dominated by the new factory system. In his opinion this was an indisputably good development, and to explain how it had come about he crafted a persuasive story about our human nature naturally leading us into a world of wage labor.

What differentiates humans from other species, Smith argued, is our ability – indeed our inclination – to engage in trade. To support his contention, Smith asks us to compare ourselves to our canine companions. Anyone can see that dogs acquire what they want (mainly food) by hunting for it or begging for it. And humans sometimes do so as well. But as a species we are unique in that we have a great many wants, and in order to satisfy them, will look to trade. "Nobody ever saw one animal by its gestures and natural cries signify to another, this is mine, that yours; I am willing to give this for that. . . . Nobody ever saw a dog make a fair and deliberate exchange of one bone for another" (Smith 1904 [1776]: sec. I.2.2).

How, though, does a general propensity to "truck, barter, and exchange" lead to a system of wage labor inside factories? Here Smith asks us to follow along on a bit of anthropological speculation. Imagine that in the distant past there was

> a tribe of hunters or shepherds [in which] a particular person makes bows and arrows . . . with more readiness and dexterity than any other. He frequently exchanges them for cattle or for venison with his companions; and he finds at last that he can in this manner get more cattle and venison, than if he himself went to the field to catch them. From a regard to his own interest, therefore, the making of bows and arrows grows to be his chief business, and he becomes a sort of armourer. (Smith 1904 [1776]: sec. I.2.3)

By specializing in a single trade, we each become expert producers who make more goods than we ourselves need. But rather than store or give away this surplus, we use it to trade with one another (eventually using money as a medium of exchange). These trades, furthermore, are pure market exchanges, as each side seeks the best deal possible for itself – we act, that is, out of what Smith refers to approvingly as "self-love."

From here it is a short step to the factory door. The principles that stimulate a division of labor *among trades* (between arrow-making and cattle-raising in the example above) eventually stimulate specialization *within trades* themselves. Smith's well-known example is of a pin factory. Formerly, a skilled craftsperson could make up to twenty pins per day. But by dividing the process into ten separate occupations, a ten-person pin factory could produce up to 48,000 pins per day. As it is highly unlikely that any worker would have need for a daily allotment of 4,800 pins, the assumption is that the factory instead gives the workers money which they can then exchange for the things they need. Hence the birth of marketized labor.

Considering how influential Smith's work remains today, it is surprising how thoroughly and repeatedly it has been refuted. We will here deal with two critiques. First, many have disputed Smith's *hollow account of human nature*. Is humanity really best defined as a species that engages in self-interested bartering? Sociolinguists, anthropologists, and biologists tend to characterize us as *Homo sapiens* rather than *Homo economicus*, emphasizing our capacity for critical thought, reflexive self-awareness, and cultural invention (Persky 1995). In this regard, time has perhaps validated an alternate vision of human nature, that of Karl Marx, who, like Smith, highlighted the uniqueness of our kind through contrast with select representatives of the animal kingdom. Like a beaver making a dam or a spider spinning a web, Marx argued, humans seem to have an inner drive to create beautiful things. But unlike animals, who are bound by instinct to produce only what they need for survival, humans have the capacity to engage in labor that is both "free" and "conscious."

To say that labor is free, in the lingo of Marxism, is to say that it is being done for reasons other than brute survival. "[M]an produces even when he is free from physical need and *only truly produces* in freedom therefrom" (Marx 1978a [1932]: 76, italics mine). To say that labor is conscious is to say that it results from a producer (or group of producers) exercising creativity, imagination, and foresight. Only a human "forms objects in accordance with the laws of beauty" (Marx 1978a [1932]: 76). To give a concrete example, imagine a man stranded in the forest who desperately assembles a basic lean-to out of some branches in order to make it through the night alive. Contrast him to a Frank Lloyd Wright or an I. M. Pei, who became architects by choice and who designed beautiful houses based on aesthetic principles. Only the latter are achieving their human potential, what Marx called our species being.

A second critique of Smith is that his theory proceeds from a *fictitious anthropology of premodern humanity*. Writing before the establishment of anthropology as a scientific field, Smith built his arguments about human nature and the ubiquity of trade around hypothetical arrow-makers and armourers. During the nineteenth and twentieth centuries, however, professional ethnologists produced a great many empirical studies of non-Western cultures (Lévi-Strauss 1992 [1955]; Malinowski 1922; Mead 2001 [1928]). Drawing on this line of research, Karl Polanyi argued that rather than being the norm, economies structured around market-based transactions are a recent and thus historically rare phenomenon. Throughout most of human history, societies utilized a variety of both formal and informal mechanisms to proscribe precisely the kind of self-interested behavior that Smith takes to be the default setting for our species. Individuals who sought to profit by explicitly haggling and bargaining with others were viewed with suspicion and would be shunned, sanctioned, or even excommunicated. In short, economic functions such as production, trade, and consumption were *embedded* within social relations (Polanyi 2001 [1944]; Polanyi et al. 1957).

Polanyi furthermore proposed a three-fold typology of embedded economic activity. The simplest system is one of *householding*, also known as autarky, from a Greek phrase meaning self-sufficient. Here, the smallest possible social unit (typically the primary group) produces and consumes the essentials of life independently, without the need for any formal systems of money or employment. And because each member will be called upon to do a wide variety of things each day, specialization will be minimal. This means that significant inventions will be rare and life generally will consist of lots of hard work. Prior to the advent of agriculture around 10,000 years ago (that is, for the bulk of the history of our 200,000+ year-old species), householding was likely the norm. But it did not die out with our nomadic hunting-and-gathering ancestors. In modern history it arises out of necessity in isolated regions such as frontiers (think of homesteads along the

Oregon Trail) and out of choice for reactionary political movements (such as the classic Transcendentalist tome *Walden*, in which Henry David Thoreau [1854] explains why he attempted to live self-sufficiently in a mountain cabin).

Another way to organize production and distribution is through *reciprocity*. Rather than engage in explicit bargaining, participants in such a system repeatedly exchange favors and gifts with each other. For example, a farmer might volunteer to help a carpenter with hauling lumber to a construction site. The following week, the carpenter returns the favor by assisting the farmer with harvesting some crops. Some weeks later a feast is held in the newly built barn for both of their families along with many neighbors. Specialization, production, and exchange have all been accomplished without the aid of wage labor. Furthermore, the exchanges that did occur were motivated not by greed and "self-love," but by sacrifice and "self-denial."[3] In extreme cases we find what anthropologists describe as a potlatch, wherein esteemed community members give away or even destroy their most valued possessions. Such acts would be considered lunacy in a market system, but in a gift economy they are perfectly sensible attempts to build trust, status, and honor.

Yet a third sort of embedded economy is one of *redistribution*. Here decisions about what is to be produced are made by a central authority, which then collects the goods and distributes them according to various non-market criteria. Centricity characterizes a variety of actual social systems, ranging from monarchies, in which a king or queen appropriates the labor of citizens through reference to divine right, to a socialist system, in which a central brain-trust preplans production to meet the population's "needs" rather than its "wants." Market activity may occur in such societies, but typically it will be small-scale and exist on the margins owing to the fact that it is morally and legally proscribed.

Given that market society is by no means natural or universal, the logical question to ask is: where *did* it come from? Polanyi himself challenged the Smithian assumption that a human propensity to barter gradually evolved into labor market institutions. He argued the converse: that the emergent market order required people to adapt their dispositions to fit it. Looking at the case of England in the eighteenth and nineteenth centuries, Polanyi argued that political intervention was responsible for forcing wage labor upon local communities by destroying the bases of their self-sufficiency. The enclosure movement, for example, turned common farming lands into private property, thereby forcing peasants to leave the countryside and seek work in the cities. A series of "poor law" reforms in turn eliminated welfare-like subsidies for the unemployed and low-skilled, again forcing people into market employment.

The sociologist Max Weber also believed that market society did not arise naturally out of human nature. But rather than a new mode of governance, Weber identified a new doctrine of religion as responsible for reversing the longstanding stigmatization of self-interest and the pursuit of profit. In *The Protestant Ethic and the Spirit of Capitalism* (Weber 2003 [1930]), he argued that for a market system of labor to function properly, employees must be motivated to work hard for high wages. But the problem is that people have traditionally been more interested in enjoying life: "A man [*sic*] does not by nature wish to earn more and more money, but simply to live as he is accustomed to live and to earn as much as is necessary for that purpose" (Weber 2003 [1930]: 60). This feeling of being content with one's lot was further buttressed by religion. Historically, practically all major faiths viewed it as sinful to be greedy and materialistic.

Weber observed, however, that Protestants in post-Reformation Europe tended to be more prosperous than Catholics, and that one particular branch of Protestantism – Calvinism – was thriving in America. He discovered that rather than proscribing selfish behavior and intense labor, Calvinism actually condoned these acts. On one hand, the religion taught adherents that the only way to please God was to engage in hard work at one's "calling." On the other hand, Calvinists believed in predestination, or the idea that one's ultimate fate (namely, whether one would go to heaven or hell) had been decided by God long, long ago. This understand-ably made the average person quite anxious. To gain some sense of relief, the Calvinist worked hard and sought to obtain material riches. This wealth would constitute a "sign" that one was indeed among the "saved"; those who exhibited indolence, by contrast, were assumed to lack grace and so were looked down upon with contempt. Thus, like both Marx and Polanyi, Weber disputed Smith's notion that self-interest is intrinsic to humankind. For this early sociologist, it was a very unique and peculiar religion that "stood at the cradle of the modern economic man" (Weber 2003 [1930]: 242).

Critiques of Capitalism

Regardless of how it arose, a capitalist system of employment soon came to constitute the norm just about everywhere on earth. In the chapters to follow we will argue that the proponents of this movement have consistently overestimated the benefits and underestimated the costs of allowing market forces alone to regulate work. As a result, they have overlooked the various ways in which commodified labor depends upon continual political intervention to function. To lay the foundation for this critique, we revisit classical debates about the overall desirability of commodified labor. Even its most strident opponents did not dispute that the great transformation had ushered in incredible gains in productivity and overall wealth. But many, observing the myriad problems that seemed to plague the new market society, wondered whether this was a Faustian bargain. In this section, we ask: What precisely is wrong with commodified labor?

For the classic liberal tradition represented by Adam Smith, this was hardly a question worth asking. The industrial revolution had ushered in a new system of production that was indisputably beneficial for both the individual and society as a whole. Consider the sections of *The Wealth of Nations* that address factory labor. Smith was well aware that many commentators saw the factory system, in which each worker does one narrow task over and over, as repellent insofar as it took well-rounded craft workers and transformed them into one-dimensional automatons. But Smith didn't see it this way at all. On the contrary, he argued, selling one's services to a factory actually improves the person, in three ways. First, it "increases very much the dexterity of the workman" (Smith 1904 [1776]: sec. I.1.6). Smith here contrasts a professional smith with a small boy working in a nail factory. The former is good at many tasks but excels at none in particular, and as a result can at best make two or three hundred nails a day. The boy, in contrast, because he applies himself to just one task, achieves excellence at it. He works with great speed and can make over two thousand nails in a day. In short, specialized labor, rather than eroding our skills, improves them.

Second, factory labor improves our work ethic. To be a craftsperson one has to constantly switch from doing one task to another. According to Smith, this introduces multiple opportunities to lose focus and become distracted: "Every country workman" soon becomes "careless . . . slothful and lazy" (Smith 1904 [1776]: sec. I.1.7). But such temptations do not exist for the wage worker, who concentrates solely on one task at a time. Such intense focus creates a third improvement in the worker: a spirit of inventiveness. "Men are much more likely to discover easier and readier methods of attaining any object," Smith argued (1904 [1776]: sec. I.1.8), "when the whole attention of their minds is directed towards that single object, than when it is dissipated among a great variety of things." He even goes so far as to claim that all industrial innovations are made not by scientists or engineers, but common workers seeking to ease their own labor. This is certainly untrue, but much like the figure of the primitive arrowmaker, the ingenious factory worker provides Smith's theory – and thus capitalism itself – with a moral legitimation.

But capitalism does not simply improve the individual worker's character. By vastly increasing the overall productivity of labor, it generates more "stuff" to be traded and thus more wealth and prosperity for society overall:

> Every workman has a great quantity of his own work to dispose of beyond what he himself has occasion for; and every other workman being exactly in the same situation, he is enabled to exchange a great quantity of his own goods for a great quantity of theirs. He supplies

them abundantly with what they have occasion for, and they accommodate him as amply with what he has occasion for, and a general plenty diffuses itself through all the different ranks of the society. (Smith 1904 [1776]: sec. I.1.10)

And if we broaden our gaze to the larger, even global, context, we see that the same process occurs. Each country will specialize in the production of those goods and services for which it holds a comparative advantage. Trade amongst countries should then allow the "general plenty" to diffuse worldwide.

Karl Marx's critique of Smith's argument was straightforward: rather than empower and enrich workers, capitalism estranges and exploits them. This message obviously resonated widely with those who actually worked in the new factory system, inspiring as it did an international movement of laborers and unions. Fundamentally, Marx disputed the notion that market labor improves our moral character. On the contrary, it would seem to contradict our very human nature as free and conscious producers. In a pure, or laissez-faire, capitalist economy, finding work on the labor market is the only way by which the mass of people can earn a means of subsistence – they work to live and not the other way around. Once one takes a job, furthermore, one typically cedes to one's employer control over what one produces and how it is produced. Neither free nor conscious, market labor *estranges* the worker from his species being. Even if we accept only a mild version of this argument (and say that work as it is currently structured falls short of maximizing our potential), we cannot but call into question Adam's Smith's optimistic vision of pin factory work as the zenith of human achievement.

Marx also challenged Smith's contention that under capitalism, a "general plenty diffuses itself" throughout society. The key issue is that of how we understand the evolution and importance of private property. It is one thing to imagine a hunter-gather who makes some arrows, claims ownership of them, and then uses or exchanges them as he pleases. But this is not the case for the factory employee. He does not leave each day with a boxful of pins! Rather it is the owner of the enterprise who is legally

entitled to claim ownership of what is produced therein. *All* of
the pins are his. To clarify the matter, Marx proposed two terms.
The forces of production, or how work is organized, are analyti-
cally distinct from the relations of production, or how ownership
is established.

Marx thus agreed with Smith that the division of labor was
improving the productivity of labor. More and more stuff, and
thus more and more wealth, was being created. But by inserting
the issue of ownership into the equation, Marx postulated a new
outcome: ever-increasing inequality. He saw that under capitalism, what is being exchanged is not the arrows I made for an equal
amount of the cattle you raised. Rather, I, a worker, sell to you,
an employer, my *capacity to work*. You, in turn, as the purchaser
of my labor power, have control over me and may rightfully claim
ownership of everything I produce. But how are the precise terms
of this exchange established? How hard must I work while under
your employ (that is, how much value I am obliged to produce),
and how large a wage will you pay me? The "dirty secret" of
capitalism as a mode of production is that it creates a dynamic
whereby the terms of this exchange will always be unequal. This
fact Marx labeled *exploitation*.

To elaborate, employers have an interest in extracting from
workers maximum effort at the lowest possible price. It is in the
nature of the game of capitalism: the firms that do so best are the
ones that make profit and survive. To make their employees work
harder and more efficiently, employers have a variety of means
at their disposal (including an ever-increasing division of labor).
Though the rate of increase may slow as the economy develops,
productivity seems to have no ceiling. Wages, in contrast, do
have a floor, which Marx refers to as the wage minimum and
which represents the bare amount of money required to sustain
a worker and the working class generally. Thus, over time,
workers produce more and more but their remuneration remains
unchanged:

> What is it that takes place in the exchange between the capitalist and
> the wage-worker? ... The worker receives means of subsistence in

exchange for his labour-power. . . . [T]he worker not only replaces what he consumes, but also gives to the accumulated labour [i.e., capital] a greater value than it previously possessed. (Marx 1978b [1849]: 125)

For Marx, the employment exchange was, at root, fundamentally iniquitous.

Polanyi surely would have agreed with this point. But his critique of the capitalist labor system was even broader. He argued that human beings are *not* commodities and that attempts to treat them as such will ultimately destroy the societies of which they are constitutive elements. Hence the dilemma. For a market order to exist, employers must have access to an abundant supply of able-bodied people available at a certain price, or wage: "Human society [must] become an accessory of the economic system" (Polanyi 2001 [1944]: 75). But this reverses millennia of taken-for-granted understandings of labor that subjugated profit-seeking behavior to social values. For Polanyi, the fact that modern labor markets were so often created through measures that intentionally destroyed traditional community life (such as poor laws, hut taxes, and enclosures) buttressed his argument that labor is a "fictitious commodity." Like Marx, he believed that the ultimate criterion by which any social system should be judged is the degree to which it serves truly human needs (such as security, companionship, or art).

Early sociologists also sought to illuminate the underpinnings and consequences of the emergent market society. Weber (1978 [1922]) believed that, whatever its origins, modern capitalism was a technically superior system that would soon crowd out alternatives. He pessimistically predicted that the rationalized profit motive represented a soulless "iron cage" in which we will remain trapped *ad infinitum*. But Émile Durkheim, whose dissertation was titled "The Division of Labor in Society," held out hope that a capitalist economy might not be incompatible with deeper moral values, the most important of which is social solidarity. Like the other critics discussed so far, Durkheim disputed Smith's notion that an increase in productivity is inherently a good thing. If specialized and marketized labor imposes great strain (what he called "fatigue") on the worker, does it really matter how much "stuff" the economy generates? As he explained:

> It is because the division of labour is accompanied by an increase in fatigue that man is constrained to seek after, as a compensatory increase, those goods of civilisation that otherwise would present no interest for him. Thus if the division of labour corresponded to no other needs than these, its sole function would be to mitigate the effects that it produces itself, one of binding up the wounds that it inflicts. (Durkheim 1997 [1893]: 158–9)

In other words, Durkheim saw Smith's vision of society as essentially masochistic – creating less and less fulfilling jobs to generate more and more pins.

What the new market economy lacked was a solid moral foundation to bind people together and make them feel that their lives had meaning. For Durkheim, the pre-market societies glorified by Polanyi, Weber, and Marx had offered their inhabitants exactly such a foundation, which he called mechanical solidarity. In these relatively small and homogeneous social groups, people had continuous personal contact with one another and formed deep attachments as a consequence. But with urbanization and industrialization, social life became more isolated and people began to feel like strangers to one another – an analysis echoed in the work of German sociologist Georg Simmel (1950 [1903]). In regards to labor, Durkheim argued that the underlying problem is that employers and workers do not understand, trust, or appreciate one another. Rather than seeing themselves as mutual dependents who would benefit from cooperation, each side acts out of self-interest (again, the contrast with Smith's theory is clear). The end result is that society exists in a pathological state with employers seeking to suppress wages, employees engaging in strikes, and everyone feeling generally unhappy. But will such a state, which Durkheim labels an "anomic division of labor," last forever? Our theorists will have a final word on the subject.

Whither Work?

What does the future hold for capitalist society and the way that it structures work? It is here that we find perhaps the greatest divergence among the theorists discussed in this chapter. At one extreme are Smith and other advocates of the emergent market society, who predicted its continuation into the indefinite future. With capitalism, they argued, we have reached the endpoint of history. At the other extreme we find Marx and Polanyi, both of whom assumed that the future would witness a radical departure from the market system. In fact, history so far has provided support for the more moderate vision of Durkheim, who correctly foresaw that modern states could and would begin to regulate the economy so as to mitigate its negative effects. To varying degrees, twentieth-century states, often prodded on by strong labor movements, moved to protect employees from the most extreme forms of alienation, exploitation, and commodification. So far into the twenty-first century, however, we find many of these protections under assault. Classical debates surrounding the future of marketized labor thus remain as relevant as ever.

For Adam Smith, a capitalist society was a great boon for humankind. It indulges our instinct to trade and barter, increases the efficiency with which we produce, improves our character, and produces great wealth for all. Its development has been responsible for civilization itself, transforming as it has "naked savages" into "industrious and frugal" workers. Given such benefits, why would society ever elect to alter course? In the Smithian paradigm, the future must be presumed to look like an elaboration of the present: ever-increasing specialization, ever-increasing trade, and ever-increasing opulence.

In such a prognostication we can discern a dichotomy between the benefits offered by trade and the threat posed by those entities that attempt to regulate or restrict it. Government, for Smith, governs best when it plays but a very minor and limited role in economic life. Of course, we should not underestimate just how revolutionary this idea was at the time Smith penned it. Seventeenth- and eighteenth-century Europe was ruled by monarchies, dictators, and despots who felt no compunction about colonizing foreign lands to extract natural resources, waging wars with one another to conquer territory, and plundering their own subjects for revenue. Indeed, the very idea of "government" (according to which leaders should protect and aid citizens much as a patriarch would care for his household) was just coming into being (Bourdieu 2004). In this context, Smith's treatise appeared as a bold document entreating those who controlled the state to leave economic activity for the most part alone.

In an oft-quoted section of *The Wealth of Nations* (1904 [1776]: sec. IV.2.9), Smith wrote:

> [Every individual] intends only his own security; and by directing [his] industry in such a manner as its produce may be of the greatest value, he intends only his own gain, and he is in this, as in many other cases, led by an invisible hand to promote an end which was no part of his intention. Nor is it always the worse for the society that it was no part of it. By pursuing his own interest he frequently promotes that of the society more effectually than when he really intends to promote it.

Smith here seems confident that, as opposed to visible interference from states (whether it be tariffs on physical goods or laws restricting the commodification of human labor), the invisible hand of the free market will best benefit society. Besides providing some rudimentary needs such as military defense and basic education, states should step aside and let markets work their magic. The future must be a capitalist one for all peoples everywhere.

For the critical tradition initiated by Marx, market society is not the endpoint of history but rather one of several stages through which humanity progresses. The strength of capitalism is that it is a dynamic system constantly generating innovations in how things are made. The market is extremely effective in this regard. By forcing businesses to compete, it stimulates them to make things more cheaply and efficiently. When it comes to distributing all this stuff, however, Marx saw capitalism to be a failure. The invisible hand doesn't so much guide us down the right path as steer us toward the edge of a cliff.

To survive, Marx argued, a firm must innovate new methods of production but also new methods to keep wages low – all the way down to the bare minimum required for survival. Even today we see innumerable examples of major companies requiring compulsory overtime, lobbying against minimum wage laws, discouraging unionization, and so on. But this introduces a contradiction. More and more goods are produced, while those who actually make them cannot afford to buy them. Unsold food and durable goods pile up in warehouses at the same time as unemployed workers go hungry on the sidewalks. We have, in short, "crises of plenty." Society may find ways to dispose of such excess supply (as when crops were dumped into the ocean during the Great Depression), but such fixes are only temporary and the problem will soon rear its head again (Harvey 2011). Thereby is exposed the fundamental flaw of capitalism. As Marx and Engels argued (1998 [1848]: 27), these "crises . . . by their periodic return put the existence of the entire bourgeois society on trial."

At the same time that the worlds of producers become increasingly disorganized and anarchic, Marx argued, the lives of workers become increasingly organized and cooperative. Wage workers (many of whom had previously been isolated rural farmers) crowd together into urban slums, while the division of labor forces them to cooperate on the factory floor. Under such conditions they begin to communicate, exchange ideas, and form a culture of their own. Before long they form trade unions and political parties, at which point we can say that workers have become a class – a proletariat – united in opposition to the class of owners that exploits them.

When conditions permit, Marx and Engels argued, workers would seize control of the economy and introduce a new system based on collective, not private, ownership of the means of production. And though they said little about how precisely work would be organized under communism, the most important fact is that human labor would no longer be bought and sold as a commodity. In addition, productivity gains would be used not to increase profit but to increase each individual's freedom by decreasing the time one must work to procure one's basic needs. With communism, "[t]he true realm of freedom, the development of human powers as an end in itself, begins. . . . The reduction of the working day is the basic prerequisite" (Marx 1993 [1894]: 959).

It is important to recognize that the Marxist account places very little faith in the power of the state to manage capitalism's failings. It is common these days to assume that more regulation equals a Marxist-style "socialism" (as *Newsweek*, on the cover of its February 2010 edition, proclaimed: "We are all Socialists Now: The Perils and Promise of the New Era of Big Government"). But the government, according to Marx and Engels (1998 [1848]), is not the agent through which capitalism will be transformed. It is not a revolutionary force but rather a tool by which capitalists maintain power. It is, they argued, "but a committee for managing the common affairs of the whole bourgeoisie" (Marx 1998 [1848]: 53). Only a movement of workers – that is, those who are direct victims of capitalist exploitation – can overthrow the system of wage labor.

Polanyi agreed with the basic thrust of Marx and Engels's argument. However, he specified a different mechanism through which capitalism would give way to an alternate future. It was not only workers, Polanyi argued, who would come to challenge the market system. Insofar as the fictitious commodification of labor threatened the moral fiber of human communities, protectionary movements could spring spontaneously from a variety of sources. Families, community groups, congregations of faith – in short, all those institutions that we now label "civil society" – had an interest in preventing people from being treated as mere commodities. Again and again, as market forces push forward, these groups push back, a process Polanyi labeled a "double movement."

And because of the diverse sources from which protectionist sentiments could spring, it was hard to say with certainty where society was headed. Surveying twentieth-century European history, Polanyi saw that movements to combat the market had led to a variety of outcomes: socialism in Russia, fascism in Italy, a "New Deal" in the United States, and so on. He himself seemed to advocate something along the lines of the cooperative communities envisioned by the industrialist Robert Owen. These were not wholesale rejections of private property or industry, insofar as employees would still produce things to be sold on the market. But workers themselves would not be treated as commodities. Employers would respect their entire social being while work itself would be embedded within a larger community context.

Looking back now from the vantage point of the early twenty-first century, it is apparent that most of these non-market alternatives failed, save one. A few small-scale cooperatives have proven tenable, but the vast majority have demonstrated short half-lives. The grand socialist experiment of the Soviet Union ended ingloriously, while China drifts further from the communist ideal with each new ten-year plan. Somewhat surprisingly from the viewpoint of classical social theory, society managed to live *with* capitalism, most notably by fostering the growth of powerful state institutions to regulate it. In fact, from among the classical theorists discussed in this chapter, perhaps Durkheim proved most prescient in his predictions of the future to come (Steiner 2010).

As described above, Durkheim believed that the problems of market society derived from insufficient regulation of the relationships among its parts. To remedy this pathological state, some part of society must come to serve as the "brain": that is, as the organ that produces nothing on its own but rather specializes in coordinating the other parts of the social body. So while premodern governments were obsessed with punishing people (in line with a negative or repressive conception of law), the modern state seeks to regulate in a positive manner what people do and how they interact with one another. In brief, the state lays a foundation for what Durkheim calls organic solidarity, a social order based upon a high degree of specialization coupled with mutual respect and cooperation among its members. In regard to industrial relations, we would expect that eventually exploitation of workers by employers would end, as would the strikes and other actions on the part of employees. This would reflect the gradual accumulation of laws, policies, and norms ensuring that workers receive fair pay and respectful treatment.

This basic insight – that states can manage market society so as to mitigate its self-destructive tendencies – established a foundation for twentieth-century social theorizing. Critical scholars such as Antonio Gramsci, Jürgen Habermas, and the thinkers associated with the Frankfurt School reinvigorated the Marxist paradigm: How does the state organize consent to capitalism? Why do regular people think of exploitative work as legitimate? In brief, how is hegemony established? Within economics, sociology, and history, it opened up the study of comparative political economy: Why do different nations manage markets so differently? Why are there so many varieties of capitalism? And for policy-makers, it has in many ways come to define the essence of modern economic governance. What mix of regulations will achieve the desired ends? Where should markets be allowed and where should they be restrained?

Curiously, Durkheim himself rarely returned to the subject of labor after the successful defense of his doctoral thesis. He became interested in culture, religion, and the mind, penning several important books on these subjects, including one that he coauthored with his student, the soon to be renowned anthropologist Marcel Mauss. Entitled *Primitive Classification* (1963 [1903]), it explored how aboriginal peoples created symbolic systems that divide the world up into discrete categories of things. Though these classification systems were social constructions, people soon tended to forget this and it thus came to seem natural and obvious that warriors were distinct from priests, hunters from nurturers, sky spirits from earth spirits, and so on. It is our contention that scholars have neglected to consider how cultural classification systems underpin modern labor markets. These systems naturalize "employment" as a taken-for-granted category, but they also serve as a terrain of struggle among those who wish to preserve or challenge the commodification of labor.

3

Classifying Labor

Having written several influential works on the origins of social security legislation, Ed Amenta, a professor of sociology at New York University (NYU), grew tired of sitting in his office all day. Reviving a passion from his youth, he began playing for and managing a softball team in Central Park, eventually becoming so obsessed with the game that he earned the nickname "Professor Baseball" (Amenta 2007). Doing sociology, we could say, was his day job insofar as he produced things (scientific articles, grant applications, course lectures) that possessed value and for which his employer (NYU) paid him. The softball league, in contrast, did not produce any significant revenues nor did it compensate players for their efforts.

At around this same time, Stephen Curry was emerging as a star college basketball player at Davidson College in North Carolina. After his junior year he left school early to enter the NBA draft, where he was selected by the Golden State Warriors and signed to a multi-million dollar contract. In 2011, the collective bargaining agreement between the labor union representing NBA players and the league's owners expired. Unable to negotiate a new agreement, the owners canceled the start of the season, leading many players to sign contracts with teams in Europe and Asia. Mr. Curry, however, decided to use this unexpected free time to finish his senior thesis and thereby obtain his sociology degree from Davidson (Bonnell 2011).

It is interesting to reflect on what these two lives can teach us about work, or, more precisely, about how a given activity comes to be thought of as work. For Mr. Amenta, doing sociological research is undoubtedly a job, but for Mr. Curry it is something else entirely: an education experience. Conversely, Mr. Curry shoots a basketball as his occupation, whereas for Mr. Amenta throwing a ball around was a fun and meaningful way to fill his free time. What is work for one is leisure for the other, and vice versa. One conclusion that we may draw from this comparison is that there is no essential characteristic of an activity that determines its status as "employment." Rather, it depends on the larger context and processes through which the activity acquires meaning.

Now one might object: "Stephen Curry pays tuition to study sociology, whereas NYU pays Ed Amenta to teach sociology. It's as simple as that. You're an employed worker if someone is paying you to do what you do." In reality, however, we observe many people who are paid for their labors, but who are not considered workers. For instance, at the same time that Professor Amenta was perfecting his swing in Central Park, graduate students at NYU were engaged in a struggle with the university (Krause et al. 2008). They were upset that despite working as teachers and research assistants, they were not considered to be employees and hence were denied the basic rights that such a status entails. Several years later, the status of graduate students at many universities across the United States remains a source of dispute: are they employees or not?

As illustrated by this example and others to be discussed in this chapter, the boundaries demarcating formal employment from various other states – leisure, management, ownership, retirement, education, crime – are continuously under dispute. Nor can such boundaries be defined as simply a question of who gets paid and who doesn't. To transform work into employment involves an alchemy that is political, cultural, and social in nature.

The previous chapter put forward the Polanyian argument that the creation of modern market society entailed the perpetuation of a fiction. This was the Smithian idea that human labor is a commodity that can be bought and sold like any other. In this chapter we examine a key process by which this fiction is continuously sustained in practice: the creation and stabilization of "employment" as a social category. In order for wage labor to exist as an institution, there must be some legally recognized class of persons who are permitted to sell their labor to others. An "employee" must exist not only as a concrete individual but also as a recognized social role. And there is no better way to observe how employment gets established as a category than to study how the boundaries of this category are created and challenged in practice.

One puzzle to emerge from this endeavor is that of unexpected responses to labor's commodification. Polanyi himself assumed that society would naturally push back against the disembedding of labor from the social: "Don't treat us as mere employees!" As the example of the NYU grad students demonstrates, however, embeddedness can work in reverse. It is quite common within capitalism to find people clamoring to have their work commoditized: "We demand to be recognized as employees!" To explain such puzzles, we should first consider some general principles of how classification works.

From Natural to Social Classification

Every day, we humans are inundated with sensations. To make sense of the myriad sights and sounds that we encounter, we need some way to sort them into different categories of things. This was a central idea of the philosopher Immanuel Kant. In works such as *Critique of Pure Reason* (1999 [1781]), he argued that the world-out-there (the noumena, in his phrase) can never be grasped directly as it is. All we can ever have is our interpretation of it – the world-as-it-appears-to-us, the phenomena. But how do humans form their impressions and interpretations of the world? Drawing on a long tradition of epistemology dating back to Aristotle, Kant argued that the mind comes pre-equipped with four built-in categories of understanding: quantity, quality, modality, and relationality. By filtering our sensations in a certain way, the categories can be said to actively create the world.

Classifying Labor

Kant's position was quite radical insofar as it challenged long-held dogma about the nature of reality and the mind. But successive scholars pushed Kant's argument even further. They maintained that the categories of understanding do not derive from the innate structure of the mind. As Durkheim and Mauss (1963 [1903]: 7) stated, "To examine the very idea of classification is to understand that man [*sic*] could not have found its essential elements in himself." One consequence of this assertion is that categories should not be universal. They should vary across groups. Durkheim and Mauss thus presented a great deal of evidence showing that various non-Western peoples utilized very different schemata to classify the things of their natural environments.

But how do certain societies come to categorize in particular ways? Ultimately, Durkheim and Mauss argued, a group's classificatory system derives from its own social structure. Clans and patriarchies thus perceive the world as divided into family units related through kinship (e.g., the sky-god mates with the sea-god); while class-based societies think in terms of ownership (e.g., man as owner of the forests). Classification, in brief, is a sociocentric rather than anthropocentric process.

The paradigm shift initiated by Kant and pushed forward by Durkheim and Mauss gave rise to a flurry of theorizing about categorization as a social process.[1] Cultural anthropology and sociolinguistics established that language is a key institution mediating between cultural categories and everyday perception. According to what is now known as the Sapir–Whorf hypothesis, the words we use to speak about our world reflect and reinforce the way we view the world. The field of semiotics further systematized the study of language as a system by which are united phonetic utterances and mental representations. The field of sociology was somewhat slow to embrace this "cultural turn" in the study of categorization. In recent decades, however, the approach has been increasingly utilized in two fields relevant for the study of marketized labor: political sociology and the sociology of markets.

If we accept categorization as a social fact, several necessarily political questions arise. How are dominant categories of thought established? Whose interests do they serve? Under what conditions are they challenged? What is the outcome of such challenges? A key insight of political sociology has been that states are the key category-makers of the modern world. As described in the previous chapter, the rise of a capitalist market economy was enabled by the emergence of national states able to exert their power over society in novel ways. The standard sociological narrative of this process highlights the state's usurpation from monarchs and feudal lords of the authority and capacity to impose military rule over a territory (Tilly 1985). As Weber (1978 [1922]) argued, states alone can claim a monopoly on the use of physical violence and police order within their territories.

But more recently, scholars have recognized that modern states possess an equally important power: they function as a "central bank of symbolic credit" (Bourdieu 1998: 376). In other words, the categories that governments use to divide up the actors and institutions of society become the common-sense categories that citizens use to see and interpret the world (Stapleford 2009). A census, for example, will establish an exclusive and exhaustive list of racial-ethnic classifications from which respondents must select an identity. Over time, these become officially recognized and taken for granted as humanity's essential and unchanging "races." A scholar could thus perform a study documenting wage differences between African–Americans and Caucasians, but he or she could also, in the words of sociologist Pierre Bourdieu (1999 [1991]), "objectify objectification": that is, document how these particular classifications came to exist in the first place.

This is precisely what economic sociologists have begun to do (Hsu et al. 2009; Navis and Glynn 2010; Rao 2009). Any market, in order to function, must contain a shared recognition of various categories of actors and actions. Some entities must be designated as legitimate sellers, some as legitimate buyers, while the product exchanged between the two must be (more or less) clearly defined and differentiated from other similar products. Such classificatory labor constitutes a large part of the routine work of modern states. When a regulatory body specifies which firms should receive business licenses or which inventions should receive patents, it is drawing upon cultural and moral principles to draw boundaries. And not surprisingly, these boundaries are frequently matters of contention. Some actors will try to enter a category; others will try to exit it; while yet others will propose entirely new schemata. Categorization within markets, in brief, is a dynamic political process.

Markets for labor should be no exception to this general principle. Over time and with a great deal of variation, capitalist states have established "employee" and "employment" as valid social (and thus mental) categories. In fact, they have been so successful in doing so that almost everyone now takes these categories for granted. According to time-use surveys, for instance, Americans now spend as much time working (i.e., doing activities that create value) at home as they do working in formal employment. Working mothers in particular are likely to engage in "second shifts" (Hochschild and Machung 1989). But collectively, Americans are socialized to not think of activities such as changing the oil in one's car, preparing dinner, or babysitting a neighbor's child as "real work" (even if they do receive remuneration for these tasks). They are simply hobbies, chores, or a "way to make ends meet."

How does a given activity come to be recognized as employment and a given person a worker? This is what sociologists call boundary work, or the contentious processes by which "conceptual distinctions [are] made by social actors to categorize objects, people, practices, and even time and space" (Lamont and Molnár 2002: 168). Although there are many different dimensions along which boundaries can be drawn around the employment category, we will focus on two (see figure 3.1). The first (vertical) dimension is about how occupations are taxonomized in a given society. It demarcates official employment from, on one hand, devalued (and often) unrecognized activities such as housework and, on the other, high-status activities such as management. The second (horizontal) dimension is about life-course demarcation. It establishes the boundaries between the condition in which one exists before entering the world of employment (e.g., education) and those that define life after employment (especially retirement).

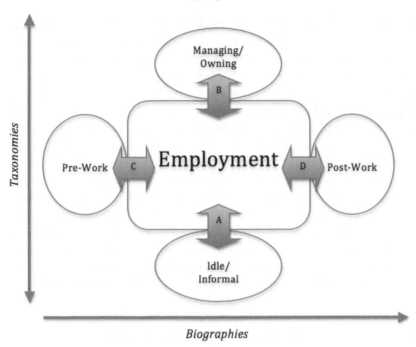

Figure 3.1 Institutional and individual boundaries of employment

Though often taken for granted, these categories are not natural and invariant. Throughout the majority of human history, for example, the elderly were expected to engage in productive activities. It was only with the establishment of the regulated economy that there formed the notion of a distinct period of life known as retirement in which one no longer has to sell one's labor on the market. The Great Recession that commenced in 2008 has in turn witnessed a lengthening of the standard working life across many countries, all in the name of austerity.

In both the establishment and unraveling of a right to retire, states have exercised their authority to draw boundaries around the employment category. But this has not meant that people and collectivities have been entirely passive. In fact, we can differentiate two sorts of active boundary work that go on all the time.

On one hand, we have *individual boundary-making*. This is the process whereby people manage their own lives in relation to the existing categories. When a worker decides to quit her job in order to start a business, or when a fresh high school graduate opts to go to college instead of taking his first job, they are negotiating categories and boundaries in the context of their own lives. On the other hand, there is *institutional boundary-making*. This refers to attempts, usually made by collectivities of actors, to shift the boundaries themselves. When a policy institute recommends shifting the retirement age from 65 to 67, or when citizens take to the street to protest this change, they engage in institutional boundary work. Both individual and institutional boundary-making demonstrate that the legitimation of a market economy requires a consensus to be established as to what sorts of work will count as employment. Categorization is a foundational process by which the market exchange of labor is both enabled and constrained.

How to Recognize a Worker

To start, we may consider the boundary separating formal employment from various work-states in which otherwise employment-eligible adults may find themselves (arrow A in figure 3.1). These would include involuntary unemployment, voluntary unemployment, work in the informal sector, unpaid household labor, forced labor, incapacitation, early retirement, and many others.

There are a variety of reasons why someone who found himself or herself in such a state would wish to move into the official category of employment. Consider the direct economic benefits to doing so. While informal work is often woefully underpaid, even a low-skilled job in the formal sector will fall under the aegis of minimum wage laws. Such laws are a key mechanism by which states protect workers from the pressure of a true free market. (Even if you live in an area with high unemployment where many people would willingly work for very low pay, the government establishes a certain basic rate below which pay cannot be set.)

Eligibility for financial support when one is incapable of working is another benefit of formal employment. States reserve the right to tax wage income, and have developed systems to distribute money to workers who have reached retirement age, have fallen ill, or who have lost their jobs and cannot find another. Again, we observe a good deal of variation in how exactly these benefits are distributed (Kenworthy 2007), while the global financial crisis that commenced in 2008 is curtailing their availability across most developed economies. But the underlying truth remains: by having one's labor classified as employment, one becomes eligible for financial support during those times when one is not in the labor market.

More generally, being recognized as an employee entitles one to claim a payment for one's services in the first place. The world is full of people who work and create value, but who are not remunerated financially at all. Consider the case of student-athletes at the collegiate level in the United States. They possess special skills that are in great demand; they are required to put in long hours of practice every week; and they generate a "product" that often translates into ticket sales, television contracts, and merchandise revenues. On the surface, one could argue that they perform work that creates immense value for their school-employers. However, the colleges they attend resolutely maintain that these are "student-athletes," not "athlete-employees," and hence are entitled to no monetary remuneration besides a tuition waiver.

The basic principle – that if one receives pedagogical benefits from one's efforts, one cannot occupy the employment status – can apply even when one *is* receiving a paycheck. This is the case for graduate students struggling to be recognized as workers. In the case of NYU discussed earlier, no one disputed that grad students perform paid work for the university. And NYU did eventually agree to negotiate a union contract with them, granting a 40 percent pay increase as well as medical benefits. But this was not the end of the story, for the university appealed to the ultimate arbiter of symbolic disputes – the state. In 2004, the US National Labor Relations Board (NLRB) ruled that because they spent so much time on their own studies, teachers and research assistants were students – and *not* workers. The union's president not surprisingly disagreed, stating, "These people obviously are workers[.] If members of the N.L.R.B. can't recognize a worker when they see one, they shouldn't be on a national labor board" (Greenhouse and Arenson 2004). Ultimately, the status of student-employees remains a matter of dispute. But as this example demonstrates, it is not a simple matter to recognize a worker when you see one.

There are reasons beyond economic ones why people can and do struggle to have their labor classified as employment. To move from unrecognized labor to formal employment is to undergo an ontological transformation. One becomes not simply a body to be bought and sold, but an industrial citizen endowed with certain inalienable rights and protections. Even if you take a job in a relatively low-skilled and low-status field (such as fast-food work), you enter into an official contract among yourself, your employer, and the state. With minimal variation across capitalist societies, such contracts provide you a right to form a union, protection from physical abuse, and compensation if you are injured on the job. They specify a maximum number of hours that your employer can require you to work daily and weekly – as well as an appropriate rate of compensation if you work overtime. They guarantee that you will be allotted a certain amount of time each day to have a meal, take a rest, and use the bathroom (Linder and Nygaard 1998). And increasingly, states mandate that employers shall not discriminate against employees or job-seekers on the basis of ascribed characteristics such as sex, race, ethnicity, religion, and age (Skrentny 2002).

The manner in which states define and count those trying to enter the labor market matters a great deal as well. Consider the unemployment rate. This is a number frequently used to interpret the overall health of an economy and to compare the relative performance of different economies. But it is not an objective indicator of an underlying reality (Stapleford 2009). Rather, it reflects a particular set of conventions for defining the boundary between employment and unemployment. Prior to the recent crisis, the United States was frequently acclaimed because of its

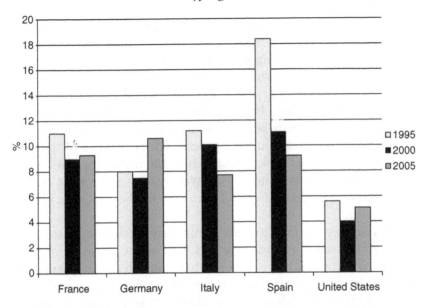

Data source: Organization for Economic Co-operation and Development, *Main Economic Indicators* 2010; Economic Policy Institute.

Figure 3.2 Unemployment rates in 1995, 2000, and 2005 for select OECD countries

unemployment rate of around 5 percent, which was low compared with peer industrialized nations of Europe (see figure 3.2). But did this really mean that 19 out of every 20 American adults were gainfully employed during these years? Not at all. For instance, the government only counts a person as unemployed if they are not working *and* are actively seeking work. Those who have been become so discouraged that they no longer even try to enter the labor market are not counted. Nor are those who desire to work in a full-time position but can only find part-time or temporary work. The United States' overall employment rate also obscures the fact that the country incarcerates a large percentage of its working-age population – especially young African-American men (Western 2007). If these individuals were to be counted among the unemployed, the United States' unemployment rate would look much more similar to that of its peer nations.

The fact that the incarcerated are typically not counted in employment statistics is ironic given that in many societies, prisoners are required to engage in labor. This leads us to consider the opposite process of that discussed so far (i.e., the downward-pointing dimension of arrow A in figure 3.1). How and why can a value-creating activity be reclassified as a form of non-work? It is useful to distinguish between two ways in which this occurs: on one hand, as an involuntary process whereby labor is "pushed out" of the realm of employment against the will of the worker; on the other, as a process whereby the worker actively seeks to escape from the employment category because he or she sees some benefit in doing so.

Let's start with the case of involuntary exclusion. Insofar as employment status endows workers with rights and benefits, it is easy to see how employers would have an interest in asking the state to classify workers' labor as something else. The case of NYU appealing to the NLRB to deny graduate students' claim to unionization is a case of such a symbolic maneuver. Another would be the widespread use of inmate labor. Throughout history, political rulers had viewed criminals as rebellious subjects deserving of (often brutal) physical punishments. A thief would have his hand cut off and be sent on his way. With the rise of market society, however, deviant activity was increasingly blamed on a poor work ethic. Thieves, trespassers, and beggars were now imprisoned and forced to engage in various forms of therapeutic labor (Foucault 1995 [1975]). It did not take long for private interests to take advantage of this captive labor pool, undoubtedly because prisoners do not qualify as official employees and so are ineligible for key rights such as a minimum wage or union representation. Hidden from the public eye today, drug offenders shell cashews on Vietnamese farms (Human Rights Watch 2011), car thieves harvest gardens in Florida (Brown and Severson 2011), while convicted murderers staff call centers in India (Burke 2011).

Globalization has created another category of workers who are involuntarily excluded from the rights of employment: undocumented migrants. Seeking a better life but unable to obtain official permission to migrate, many denizens of the global South furtively cross borders in search of work. There they encounter employers in competitive and labor-intensive sectors such as agriculture, construction, and textiles who are only too happy to hire them. And why not? Because they lack citizenship, undocumented workers have difficulty claiming even the most basic of protections afforded recognized employees. To make such appeals to the state would risk exposing oneself to arrest, detention, and deportation. An undocumented worker must by necessity perform invisible labor. Employers can and do take advantage of this fact, by paying sub-minimum wages and committing other acts that would be deemed illegal according to standard labor law (Bonacich and Appelbaum 2000).

Those whose very persons are deemed illegal may be forced to work in the shadows. The same holds if the labor you perform is deemed unacceptable by social standards (and even if a demand for it exists). Prostitution is commonly called the world's oldest profession, meaning that the ability of one person to perform sexual services for another has historically been a value-producing act. By our definition, it constitutes a form of work. But with few contemporary exceptions (e.g., the Netherlands and the US state of Nevada), prostitution is *not* deemed work, but rather a criminal act. As a result, those who engage in it have few legal protections and are often mistreated by their clients, their pimps, and even the police (Rosen and Venkatesh 2008). Many scholars debate whether prostitutes should be thought of as "sex workers" engaged in "erotic labor." But this misses the point insofar as it is ultimately not up to academics to decide upon such classifications. It would be immensely more beneficial to study the *actual processes* through which activities such as the provision of sexual services are categorized as criminal vices rather than legitimate employment (Bernstein 2007).

As the examples of prostitutes and undocumented migrants suggest, the boundary between acknowledged and unacknowledged work is gendered and raced. This reflects cultural stereotypes that are deeply entrenched in state actors and state institutions. A census, for example, is an instrument of modern governance, executed every five or ten years, that takes stock of the population. By surveying people about their identities and activities, however, a census can be said to construct and bound certain categories, including employment. One issue that planners of a census must confront is how to classify those who engage in productive labor in the household. Tasks such as caring for children, doing laundry, and cleaning (what Marx called the labor of social reproduction) are very important, but they have historically been designated as "women's work." With the rise of a capitalist market economy, they were further devalued because they did not directly produce cash income for the household (Illich 2000 [1981]; Oakley 1984). As Ann Crittenden (2001: 45) demonstrates, male government officials in the nineteenth century made the decision to reclassify housewifery from a legitimate occupation into a general state of idleness; with the removal of a checkbox on a census form, the work of millions of women was "disappeared."

Similarly arbitrary distinctions were drawn around domestic and agricultural workers in the United States, where many of the key protections discussed so far originated with a series of initiatives put forward by President Franklin D. Roosevelt and collectively dubbed the New Deal. The Social Security Act of 1935, for instance, established a national insurance fund for retired and disabled workers; while the Fair Labor Standards Act of 1938 established a minimum wage, specified the standard work-week, and proscribed child labor (Murray 2010). In order to pass such legislation through Congress, however, Roosevelt agreed to exclude several occupational categories in which African–Americans were (and continue to be) heavily represented. Domestic employees such as home health care aides, for example, were not considered employees because they provide only "companionship" rather than anything of actual value.

Not even such a tenuous justification was offered for removing agricultural workers from the employment category. They were excluded merely to appease business and political interests in the US South. Following the North's victory in the Civil War, Southern landowners could no longer use slavery as a source of free labor. In its place they instituted a system of sharecropping whereby newly free but still impoverished and landless African–Americans were allowed to occupy and farm the land. But in return the freedmen had to turn over a good portion (usually half or more) of the crop, and also repay any debt incurred in the process of planting. Had agricultural workers been classified as employees under Roosevelt's New Deal legislation, the system of sharecropping would have collapsed. One month of social security insurance would have provided a freedman more income than an entire year of sharecropping, thereby undermining the cycle of debt and peonage that reproduced the social standing of landed white elites (Quadagno 1994). Well into the twentieth century, then, a feudal system of labor survived insofar as certain activities of farming were classified as something other than employment proper.

Given the many benefits and rights to be gained by having one's work categorized as employment, it may seem counterintuitive that one would actively strategize to avoid such a classification. But this is not uncommon. According to the Organization for Economic Co-operation and Development (Jutting and de Laiglesia 2009), about half of all the world's workers are found outside of the realm of official employment categories. Many of these surely would like to be formally recognized. But there are also benefits to working below the radar, so to speak. First, one may be a legal person engaged in a legal trade, but still wish to avoid paying taxes or other deductions on one's earnings. Divorced men who have alimony or paternity payments automatically taken from their paychecks, for instance, may actively seek to find work "under the table." Second, one might seek to disguise the true nature of one's work from the state or other authorities. This would be the case for a political activist engaged with organizing a protest against an authoritarian government. It would very much be in that person's interest to have his or her daily work-tasks perceived as "visiting neighbors" as opposed to "inciting rebellion." Third, one could avoid being formally classified as an employee in order to keep one's very person invisible. This is the case for felons who face warrants for their arrest but must still find a way to earn money while living "on the run" (Goffman 2009).

More Than a Job

We now turn our attention to the symbolic labor that occurs at the upper boundary of the employment category (arrow B in figure 3.1). Actually, the elaboration of classifications above and beyond employment would have surprised classical thinkers such as Marx, who predicted that capitalism would quickly polarize the social structure into two classes: a small minority of property-owners, with the vast majority reduced to wage laborers.[2] In fact, as capitalism advanced and as states began to regulate the economy, new sorts of occupational categories came into being. Those who occupy these positions perform work in a general sense. But in reality, boundaries are often drawn between mundane employment and these higher-status categories, three of which we will consider here: management, professions, and entrepreneurs.

Early in the history of capitalism, most businesses were relatively small and owned by individuals or families. Proprietors, with the assistance of a select group of foremen, personally monitored the production process. In addition, work was often contracted to intermediaries who were then responsible for the procurement and monitoring of workers (known as the putting-out system). As markets grew in size, so did firms, which now contained not only workers but also vast numbers of managers who did not produce anything themselves but rather administered the running of the enterprise (Chandler 1977; Simon 1997a [1945]).

From the start it was recognized that managers have their own identities and interests separate from those of workers and owners. Management even eventually became its own field of study in colleges and universities (Khurana 2010). And perhaps most significantly, management became taken for granted as a social category. In the vernacular it was denoted as "white-collar," meaning that those who inhabited the category would wear a plain (and clean) dress shirt as opposed to the workman's "blue-collar" uniform. Meanwhile, most legal systems came to recognize managers as a distinct occupation. Government surveys of businesses now routinely inquire as to which personnel are managers, executives, administrators, and so on.

At first glance, the boundary work between management and employment seems easy to comprehend. At an institutional level, we would simply define managers as those who supervise workers, and workers as those who actually work. And at the individual level, it would make sense that those who reside in the employment category would have an interest in attempting to rise up into the world of management. Better wages and less work await! But once again, the social embeddedness of employment complicates matters. In the real world, jobs often entail a mixture of both productive and supervisory activities. An executive might spend hours writing a report, while a veteran worker watches over a new-hire. To impose a bounded category upon the fuzzy texture of organizational life entails isolating and prioritizing some aspects of a given role. Nor is this process arbitrary. It occurs in line with cultural conventions and political considerations – the latter taking prominence especially when tangible stakes are involved.

To give one example of the political embeddedness of the manager–employee boundary, we may consider the case of nurses in the United States. Since the beginning of modern medicine, they have been considered a "pink-collar" proletariat – skilled workers who are nonetheless obligated to carry out the orders of physicians (Chambliss 1996). In recent years, however, various aspects of care have been routinized and delegated to low-cost personnel, often referred to as nursing aides. To preserve their wages and working conditions, many nurses have opted to join labor unions. This in turn provoked an interesting response by many hospital administrators: they began to reclassify nurses as managers on the grounds that nurses now supervised the work of the aides who were replacing them. This mattered because according to the relevant labor law, only employees – *and not supervisors* – are entitled to form labor unions. As with the case of graduate students, this spurred a flurry of lawsuits and countersuits. Here the underlying boundary dispute was not one of non-workers pushing their way into the employment category, but rather one of established employees resisting an involuntary exit from the category.

The professions represent a second category often distinguished from the ranks of regular employment. Architects, psychologists, and surgeons are examples of professionals who provide services of great value, and who usually receive ample compensation in return. But it is not a smooth gradation from wage worker to salaried professional. Engineers do not simply earn a bit more and have a few more years of education than mechanics. According to Abbott (1988), professionals represent a historically novel type of worker that applies abstract knowledge to specific problems. This necessarily entails prolonged training to enter a profession, as well as a dedicated system for maintaining the profession's knowledge base (in the form of schools, certificates, associations, codes of ethics, journals, etc.). As modern society became increasingly dependent upon science and technology, the relative power of the professions grew in turn. Many scholars have claimed that they constitute a "new class" of technocrats who exercise power over society at large (Eyal and Buchholz 2010).

The process of professionalization is a prime example of contested categorization. According to Abbott, professions can claim a legitimate identity only after first battling and dominating other social groups. In order to monopolize the treatment of mental illness, psychologists had to dispute the expertise of traditional healers, prison wardens, and exorcists. As a result of such victories, the professional category comes to be associated with a high degree of social honor.

Gutek (1995) argues that professionals, like basic service workers, often deal with clients in a face-to-face manner. But a lawyer, unlike a butler, will command respect and deference from service-recipients. It is therefore not surprising to find that many workers who may not technically qualify will nonetheless seek to classify their work as professionalism. In an ethnographic study of a South African leisure resort, Sallaz (2010) found that workers felt embittered by the poor treatment they received from management. At a staff meeting he attended, one worker stated publicly that: "I am here to be a service professional . . . if I am not happy then the guest is not happy!" Sherman (2005) found similar acts of claim-making among service staff in US luxury hotels. Even though they had no chance of having room-cleaning or drink-serving officially reclassified as a profession, maids and waiters still sought to push themselves across the boundary separating respected expertise from brute labor.

Between Childhood and Retirement

Up to now we have examined how employment is stabilized as a category within an *institutional taxonomy*. By delineating specifically which occupations and activities count as "work," states define the boundaries of labor markets. We now consider a second dimension along which employment is established as a category: the *individual biography*. In regulated capitalism, employment is confined only to particular stages of the life span. This is a perfect example of embedding in that institutions of civil society have reacted against the logic of the market to limit the extent to which human labor is commodified. But where exactly are these protective boundaries drawn between work and, on one hand, childhood (arrow C in figure 3.1) and, on the other, retirement (arrow D in figure 3.1)? And how do people actually negotiate these boundaries in their lives?

Before market society, *childhood* did not exist. This does not mean that humans did not mate and generate offspring. It just means that in order for there to be an idea of childhood as a distinct stage of life, it had to be contrasted with some other stage – namely, employment. In Europe prior to the nineteenth century, there was no real distinction between home and the workplace. On a family farm, for instance, all members of the household (including children) would engage in productive activity, while the boundaries among labor, rest, and leisure were often fuzzy. When labor markets first emerged, this longstanding pattern persisted as children went out to work in factories and mines, often alongside their parents. Even if children stayed at home, they would engage in market labor to help their parents complete tasks sent home with them by their employers – the original meaning of the phrase "homework."

Eventually the category of employment was bounded at its

lowest end to exclude those deemed children. This was the result of two processes. The first was the expansion of compulsory education at the primary and secondary levels (Meyer et al. 1992). Advocates argued that successful democratic governance required a literate population, and thus that basic education should be a component of modern citizenship. To the extent that children spent their days in the workplace, they were precluded from attending school. A second force against child labor was a powerful social reform movement protesting that child labor was inherently inhumane and abusive. During the nineteenth and early twentieth centuries, many countries implemented laws setting a minimum age at which one can be employed. In 1973, the International Labor Organization (ILO), a specialized agency of the United Nations, established an international standard. The ILO's Minimum Age Convention specified the age of 15 years as the lowest at which a person could be employed under normal conditions. Attesting to the fact that this is still very much a boundary in dispute, the ILO also estimates that there are well over 200 million child workers worldwide today.

For the individual who lives in a regulated market economy, there are two key choices to make about negotiating the boundary between "childhood" and labor. First is the decision about *when* to cross the boundary – that is, when to leave school and begin full-time work. One can opt to enter work immediately upon meeting the minimum age requirement and before obtaining a secondary degree (a high school diploma or the equivalent); one can seek employment after obtaining a secondary degree; or one can delay finding a career until after completing some post-secondary training (such as an associate, bachelors, masters, or doctoral degree). Second is the choice of *which* vocation or field to prepare for. Most likely you were asked as a child: "What do you want to be when you grow up?" The underlying message of such a question is that people should introspect and decide what type of worker they would like to be. For those who enroll in college or university, this is reflected in the requirement to pick a major: will you go into French literature or microbiology? By now a sizable body of research demonstrates that both of these decisions are consequential for one's eventual earnings and happiness (Gerber and Cheung 2008).

Explaining how people actually make such decisions reveals a sharp distinction between market theories and an economic-sociological perspective. According to the former, a person should strive to make himself or herself as valuable as possible on the labor market. The phrase "investing in one's human capital" illustrates perfectly this idea. What eventually sorts and stratifies people into different fields, according to this argument, are one's natural talents and abilities. Those with intelligence and perseverance rise to the top, while others must content themselves with society's low-paying and low-status jobs.[3] The market perspective, in short, is one of meritocracy or, if you will, social Darwinism.

In contrast, a critical economic-sociological perspective maintains that the series of decisions eventually culminating in employment remain embedded: that is, they are shaped by social factors such as cultural norms, family expectations, and resource constraints. Notably, Adam Smith, the theorist most closely associated with the market perspective, advocated the latter position. In his words, "The difference between the most dissimilar characters, between a philosopher and a common street porter . . . seems to arise not so much from nature, as from habit, custom, and education" (Smith 1904 [1776]: sec. I.2.4).

A great deal of empirical research has given support to the embeddedness perspective. For instance, the sociologist Pierre Bourdieu demonstrated that schools do not sort students according to natural intelligence; rather, they serve as a mechanism by which wealthy families reproduce their social position (Bourdieu and Passeron 1977). Middle- and upper-class parents teach their children from a young age to think independently and be conversant in subjects of art and culture. Poor and working-class parents, in contrast, implicitly teach children to follow orders and cherish material security (Lareau 2003). Educators in turn mistake these early socialization experiences as indicators of a student's inherent intelligence and giftedness. Privileged students are then guided into a college track, poor students into vocational programs, and social stratification is reproduced.

Even when teachers attempt to break this cycle, social and cultural forces come into play. This was the argument of Paul Willis in *Learning to Labor* (1981), an ethnography of working-class boys at a high school in Britain. Teachers at this school were aware of the negative effects of tracking, and intentionally tried to steer the boys into college preparatory courses. But surprisingly, the students rejected the opportunity to escape the blue-collar world. They viewed factory life as macho and exciting, and white-collar work as effeminate and stultifying; hence they would skip class and cause trouble rather than study hard and be good students. If we think of these young men as potential commodities, this was an irrational choice – especially knowing what we do now about the imminent decline of manufacturing in Britain. They passed up the chance to improve their human capital. But Willis's findings make perfect sense from the embeddedness perspective. Social factors such as gender identity, family loyalty, and a sense of solidarity with one's "mates" ultimately shaped choices about how and when to cross the threshold from childhood to labor.

This leaves but one more boundary to consider (arrow D in figure 3.1). As with childhood, we would be to correct to say that *retirement* can not exist as a social and cognitive category without being juxtaposed to employment. In pre-market societies, where life expectancy was low and medical care unsophisticated, the aged were expected to engage in useful labor (from governance to farming to childcare) until they were incapacitated or dead. The early stages of capitalism saw a continuation of this pattern. It was only with the rise of regulated capitalism that social protections were instituted to provide the material foundation for a period of respite after a life of labor.

As a category, retirement dates back to the late nineteenth and early twentieth centuries. In response to the growing power of trade unions and socialist parties, many governments offered material concessions to workers, including retirement pensions (Orloff 1993). Germany in 1883 set 65 years as the proper age for retirement, and this general standard has since become the norm. When the United States passed its Social Security Act in 1935, for example, 65 was made the age at which one can begin collecting full benefits (Amenta 2000). The results were dramatic: while 74 percent of American men over the age of 65 worked in the labor market in 1890, by 1990 only 18 percent did (Costa 1998). Today, while variation does exist in terms of the normative retirement age – Italy sets it at 60, Norway at 67 – the vast majority of citizens now take for granted the right to voluntarily remove themselves from the labor market at a certain point in their lives. Attesting to how deeply entrenched are such categories, witness the mass protests in response to recent attempts by governments to change (i.e., raise) the retirement age. The work of bounding retirement as an institutional category is a contentious and ever-ongoing project.

For the individual within regulated capitalism, a decision must be made as to how and when to cross the boundary from wage labor into retirement. Unlike the period of pre-work education (in which one accumulates human capital), there is no obvious instrumental goal of this post-work period. The retired person is being rewarded for years of labor. He or she may now relax, travel, spend time with the family, or indulge a hobby. The decision to voluntarily retire thus hinges on two things: first, how much the individual values extra leisure relative to the satisfaction from work that he or she is forsaking; second and related, the material resources available to support life after employment, such as those deriving from public entitlements, private pensions, personal savings, and social networks (especially children). These in turn depend upon future trends that cannot be known in advance, such as the inflation rate, the performance of the stock market, fluctuating health care costs, and one's expected longevity.

The resurgence of neoliberal ideology during the last decades of the twentieth century, along with the global financial crisis of the early twenty-first, has destabilized the retirement category. On one hand, many governments have sought to deal with budget crises and projected shortfalls in pension funds by pushing back the retirement boundary. Even France and Spain – two European countries with strong protectionist traditions – have proposed to raise the retirement age to 67 years. On the other hand, many companies are finding ways to induce their employees to retire early. This latter phenomenon is especially common in industries where collective bargaining agreements guarantee workers job security, annual wage increases, and generous benefits. In 2004, for instance, the US auto firm General Motors offered *all* of its 100,000-plus hourly employees a financial incentive to quit their jobs. Within two years, over a third of its workers had accepted the offer. Blue-collar workers who have spent years of arduous labor on the assembly line are often only too happy to adjust their own personal boundaries between employment and retirement (Milkman 1997).

The case of worker "buyouts" further illustrates the embeddedness of employment as a social category. Why, we might ask, would a company have to buy out a worker in the first place? Wouldn't it be much easier to simply fire him or her (especially in the United States, where a legal principle known as "employment at will" specifies that employment is a voluntary relationship that can be terminated by either party at any time)? In fact, more and more states are passing regulations specifying that firms cannot fire workers because of how old they are. For instance, the United States' Age Discrimination in Employment Act, passed by Congress in 1986, established that a person's age could not be used as grounds for dismissal. This increased workers' awareness of the issue to the point that during the 1990s, about half of all complaints made to the US Equal Employment Opportunity Commission charged an employer with age discrimination. Most buyout agreements thus require workers to sign a waiver against future discrimination claims. From the employer's perspective, then, a contractually agreed-upon retirement is not simply a way to minimize the wage bill; it is a political mechanism for maintaining the firm's reputation and precluding litigation.

In this chapter we have considered several cases in which workers struggle to enter the employment category (i.e., to have their labor commodified) in order to receive the legal protections that modern states accord formal employment. In addition, by establishing boundaries among the categories of employment, childhood, and retirement, states protect people from the pressures of commodification. No one should have to sell themselves on the labor market from cradle to grave. Both education and retirement, furthermore, are bound up with issues of compensation. If a young person is to imagine herself as a commodity, how best is she to prepare for the labor market ahead? If an aging worker is desiring release from wage labor, how can he be assured that he can support himself in the years of retirement? In the following chapter we turn our attention to the question of how particular forms of work come to be assigned particular values.

4

Commensurating Labor

Prior to 2010, most people had never heard of Taiwan's Hon Hai Precision Industry Company. For years it had been supplying components to many of the world's most well-known computing and mobile companies, including Dell, Hewlett Packard, Nokia, and Apple. But because of the complex nature of modern supply chains, the company itself remained in the shadows. This all changed, however, when between January 23 and May 25, 2010, nine workers at its Chinese subsidiary, Foxconn, killed themselves by jumping from windows. Once news of the suicides became public, an international outcry was heard from human rights groups and labor activists. Company executives responded with a variety of measures. Some, such as the installation of netting around its factories and dormitories to catch would-be jumpers, were roundly mocked as largely symbolic and most certainly *post hoc*. But somewhat surprisingly, Hon Hai did agree to give the vast majority of its workers a significant raise, of approximately 66 percent (Dean 2010).

The case of the raises at Foxconn itself raises interesting questions about how a worker's worth is determined. Had workers been underpaid prior to the spate of suicides? Their base rate of about $4 a day was only a fraction of what manufacturing workers receive in North America or Western Europe. And it was certainly miniscule in relation to the value of the laptops, cell phones, and iPods that the workers produced. But, on the other hand, the cost of living is much lower in this part of the world, nor did this rate violate China's own minimum wage standards. And Foxconn certainly had no problem finding approximately a million workers to staff its China factories! From a strict market-based perspective, if an adequate number of sellers and buyers are able to agree on a wage, it is by definition fair. But if so, why did the company agree to raise the rate? Was it simply a cynical move to preserve the company's image? Or was an alternate (i.e., non-economic) principle of valuation being acknowledged?

The previous two chapters introduced some fundamental aspects of marketized labor: chapter 2 recounted the historical process (i.e., the great transformation) by which labor came to be imagined as a commodity, while chapter 3 analyzed the mechanisms (boundary-making) by which employment becomes a legitimate social category. We now turn to the issue of how the commodification of labor is accomplished via practices of commensuration and valuation. While standard models of supply and demand can explain quite well temporal fluctuations in things such as average wages, these models typically neglect the political, technical, and normative foundations of exchange (Geertz 1978). As two leading economic sociologists state it: "Moral values can block markets. However, [they] also contribute to the value of products" (Beckert and Aspers 2011: 7). They do so by contributing to the establishment of a consensus as to what exactly is being exchanged when an employer and an employee interact, as well as the logic that will structure the exchange so as to make it fair. Commodification, in short, relies on commensuration.

Establishing Value

As with categorization, the study of valuation has a long pedigree. Dating back to ancient Greece, philosophers have sought to understand how we can judge a substance's goodness, beauty, and worth. In concrete situations of trade and barter, this is an issue of commensuration, or establishing an equivalency between two different classes of things (Espeland and Stevens 1998). If I have a stack of old books, and you have just baked a batch of cookies, we might agree to make a swap. But how many cookies equal a book? Does it matter if the story was an award winner, or if the binding on the book is coming apart? What if the cookies are made from scratch, and from a secret family recipe to boot? Historically, people tended not to explicitly haggle about these issues, but instead relied on custom and tradition to guide exchange (Graeber 2011). When, for various reasons, money became institutionalized as a medium of exchange, questions of value became questions of pricing. How do we give a good or service a quantitative notation? What does something cost?

Economics and economic sociology offer two different answers to these questions. Both reject philosophical traditions that consider value to be an inherent and immutable characteristic of an object. But the field of economics typically views the market as the ultimate arbiter, with worth emerging from the myriad decisions of actual market participants. Every potential buyer, in this perspective, has his own opinion as to how much he desires a particular thing and how much he expects it to increase his overall happiness. This is referred to as a commodity's utility. Creators of a good then adjust their production accordingly, with the equilibrium between these forces of demand and supply crystallized, if but momentarily, as the good's price. But does this model accord with reality? Economic sociologists have produced a large amount of empirical work demonstrating that valuation is a social as much as an economic process (Smith 1990; Yakubovich et al. 2005). Culture, politics, and institutions, they argue, all influence how goods are produced, desired, and priced.

Culture provides the broad foundation on which value is established. All human groups have deeply held beliefs about what is good and sacred; even in market economies, these beliefs influence how particular things become commodities. Thus, while the price of beef rises and falls in the United States in accord with the changing tastes (and health concerns) of consumers, in Hindu culture, cows are assumed to be the incarnation of deities and thus their circulation is restricted. Conversely, while many cultures have no problem with the sale of canines for meat, others treat dogs as *de facto* family members whose purchase for the purpose of eating is prohibited (and even though markets do exist to buy specialty breeds as status symbols). Attempts to put quantitative prices on things deemed invaluable entail disputes, negotiation, and what Becker (1997 [1963]) referred to as moral entrepreneurship. Zelizer (1981) showed this to be the case for the establishment of a market for children's life insurance, and Healy (2006) for attempts to allow market pricing of human blood and organs. In each case, proponents of the market logic had to alter the meanings imbued by other "economies of worth" (Boltanski and Thévenot 2006).

Pierre Bourdieu developed a framework to theorize how such valuation struggles take place. He argued that as specific domains of modern society become powerful and autonomous, they are able to create their own standards of value. Institutions of education reward linguistic competency and artistic imagination (what Bourdieu calls cultural capital); the business and financial sectors valorize those who can increase revenues and profits (economic capital); research institutions prize innovative thinking about cutting-edge issues (scientific capital); and so on. Rather than a static typology, Bourdieu proposed a dynamic model of how forms of capital increase or decrease in value relative to one another. Key to this process is the idea of a "field of power," a privileged institutional space wherein there occurs a "struggle for power among different species of power" (Bourdieu 1998: 264). The outcome at any given moment of this struggle can be represented as a hierarchy of legitimate principles of valuation. This can be observed in how a society answers questions such as: Who is more qualified for the presidency: a businessman or a professor? How to determine the best film of the year: the one with the most ticket sales or the one most critically acclaimed? Is it better to be rich or to be well read?

The ascendency of market-based criteria for evaluating worth, economic sociologists argue, is due in large measure to the elaboration of new technologies of quantification and measurement (Callon et al. 2002). As social groups become larger and more differentiated, the task of governing them becomes increasingly difficult. Those who aspire to rule will be drawn to forms of valuation that allow complex issues to be simplified and that permit the ready comparison of very different phenomena. The problem with aesthetic, cultural, and ethical criteria, however, is that they require sensitivity to the uniqueness of individual cases. They also typically require evaluators to take the time to become experts in their respective fields.

In contrast, the concept of utility, so central to the field of economics, reduces all such complications down to a single statement: "How much is something desired? This is its worth." As a telling example, consider the work of Fourcade (2011) on a massive oil spill by the Exxon company off the coast of Alaska in 1989. In subsequent litigation, government officials and public interests had to figure how to calculate reparations for the incident. But how to place a value on the environment? Ask a hunter, a hiker, and a hermit, and you will get three different answers appealing to three different cultural principles. With the concept of (passive) utility, all three of these views (and countless others) can be made commensurate: simply survey people and ask them directly how much, in dollars, they would be willing to pay to preserve a clean environment. Average and aggregate the responses and you now have the "cost" of an oil spill in one single number.

When it comes to labor, it is usually not necessary to estimate supply and demand hypothetically. In modern market societies, production is accomplished via myriad everyday exchanges between employers and employees. Government surveys and censuses in turn reveal the average "price" of labor across various sectors and regions. But this should not fool us into assuming that the commensuration of labor is purely an economic process. Exchange can only occur if both parties agree as to what the seller is providing, what the buyer is providing, and how an exchange rate is established between the two. The remainder of this chapter will elaborate upon the social embeddedness of these three dimensions of labor commensuration.

An Ontology of Labor

When you accept a job, what exactly are you selling to your employer? Certainly not your flesh-and-blood person – this would be tantamount to slavery, which is now officially banned in all countries. It at first makes sense to suppose that the work you do produces value, which is then remunerated accordingly. But in reality, the value of what you produce is often not known until well after the work is done and the paychecks are handed out. For example, when in 2010 the Japanese company Toyota recalled 1.5 million automobiles because of an engineering flaw, the value of the work that had been performed by those who designed and assembled the cars was greatly reduced, if not negated. But the firm did not require workers to retroactively take pay cuts or return their wages.

Marx sought to clarify the issue by distinguishing between use value and exchange value. Under all economic systems, tangible goods have a subjective (use) value from the moment they are made; but under capitalism, they acquire a monetary (exchange) value only after they have been purchased on the market. Starting from this insight, Marx argued that what employees actually sell is their *labor power*: that is, their potentiality to engage in labor. When she accepts a job, a worker basically agrees to give a certain period of time each day to her employer, who must then organize her work and ensure that she exerts the appropriate effort. The concept of labor power, in this sense, underpins the entire science of management! Chapter 6 will consider systematically the various techniques used by employers to extract effort from employees. But it is important to recognize that insofar as modern capitalism is a diverse system, there are other ways in which labor can be commoditized. From the system's beginning, alternatives to the idea of labor power have grounded the employment exchange, while in recent times the economy has evolved to encompass forms of labor besides simple physical effort.

Contrary to Marx's claims, not all capitalist societies imagine the employment relation as the sale of labor power. In a fascinating work of historical sociology, Biernacki (1995) demonstrated that nineteenth-century Germany (where Marx was residing when he penned several of his foundational works) was an outlier in terms of thinking of labor as potential effort. In England (along with France and Italy), established feudal ideas of labor as the exchange of a finished product persisted. These cultural assumptions in turn shaped the organization of work on the shopfloor itself.

In his detailed case studies of woolens manufacture, Biernacki described how British employers would allow employees discretion in terms of how they did their work, but would fine them retroactively if their products reached substandard prices on the market. German employers, in contrast, monitored workers closely and fined them for negligent behaviors at their looms; but once the wool reached the market, they were no longer considered to be responsible for its value. Similar cultural differences influenced the spatial organization of the workplace, the logic of remuneration, and even the ways in which workers would strike against their employers.

We would be correct to say that the ideal exemplified by the German system – employment as the exchange of labor power – disseminated to become the dominant one today. In regards to the substantive content of what a worker is expected to provide, however, we find not a narrowing but an expansion of the category. In brief, the idea of labor as physical exertion has given way to the idea that workers are expected to sell (and be remunerated for) their intellectual and emotional efforts. At the risk of ossifying boundaries among aspects of human effort that are in practice overlapping and coterminous, we propose that modern capitalism commodifies not only the body, but also the mind and the soul.

Sweat is often used to describe figuratively the notion of work. To have a job is to be paid to make, modify, repair, move, or dispose of actual things. One's body, furthermore, is the ultimate instrument through which such transformations of the material world are accomplished. This was certainly the case in capitalist societies during most of the nineteenth and twentieth centuries. First agriculture, and then manufacturing, made up the bulk of a typical society's gross domestic product. Even as specialized tools and machinery grew in sophistication and displaced many of the more tedious aspects of work, there was no doubt that one's body was on the line when it came to performing wage labor.

Commensurating Labor

Consider the following anecdote from Burawoy's (1979a: 87–8) ethnography of a Chicago machine shop:

> One of my jobs, which I particularly disliked, involved drilling 3/16-inch holes twelve inches deep into steel "slides.". . . After cutting a short depth, the drill would jump up to bring out chips, plunge back in again to drill another short depth, and so on until the hole was complete. Once started, the jumping jack continued automatically until the hole was finished. Because the drills were long and sometimes dull, they frequently broke, and, if they were not caught in time, the pressure could send pieces of steel flying in all directions. The job was not only dangerous but frustrating. . . . The job gave me the jitters, and I never even tried . . . preferring to stay alive and psychologically healthy.

As this illustrates, a manufacturing worker must exercise both mental acumen (knowing how to operate the drill) and emotional fortitude (managing the fear of injury). But these were really secondary or supporting aspects of Burawoy's job as a drill operator. Both employer and employee assumed that the primary purpose – that is, what Burawoy was ultimately getting paid for – was to produce a piece of steel with certain technical specifications.

Across capitalist societies, the latter half of the twentieth century witnessed a decline in manufacturing relative to service and knowledge industries. The latter entail different assumptions as to what it is that employees are commodifying and selling to their employers. Consider the service sector. As Hochschild (1983) explained, its workers are paid to provide "emotional labor," meaning that they are expected to present a certain expressive appearance in order to invoke a certain feeling in an organization's clientele. So while an airline mechanic is paid to make sure that an aircraft's engine is working properly, a flight attendant is paid to convince passengers that this is in fact the case. The mechanic may need to muster bravery in order to ascend ladders, but there can be little doubt that his employer is paying him to physically maintain the plane. Conversely, while the flight attendant may physically push a food cart up and down the aisle, her ultimate task is to project a calm and comforting aura that transforms the plane's

73

interior into a dining and resting space. In service industries, the ultimate product is not a tangible object (Whyte 1948), but rather "a state of mind" (Hochschild 1983: 6).

The astute reader may have noticed that the above paragraph used gender-specific language, with a masculine pronoun describing the mechanic and a feminine one describing the attendant. This was intentional, to highlight how the actual doing of emotional labor remains stereotyped as a feminine task. This has implications for inequality insofar as the effort emotional labor entails is often invisible, hard to quantify, and not properly rewarded. It is, in Marx's terminology, fetishized. Consumers experience and appreciate it, but are not able to fully comprehend the effort that goes into its production in the first place.

Indeed, Hochschild pointed out that service workers are increasingly required to give *authentic* feeling displays. (As one airline's motto stated, "Our smiles are not just painted on.") But to the extent that a service worker's emotional displays are perceived by the client as natural, they cease to be recognized as the deliberate application of effort. Behind the scenes, emotional laborers may be feeling dissonance (i.e., a disconnect between how they act and how they really feel) and experience burnout. But this goes unrecognized owing to the peculiar essence of emotional labor as an invisible commodity.

In the decades since the publication of Hochschild's groundbreaking study, scholars have turned their attention to two types of feminized service jobs that are growing rapidly: care work and aesthetic labor. The former entails providing for the physical and especially the spiritual needs of those who are incapacitated. A nanny caring for a toddler, a nurse attending to a sick patient, and a hospice worker comforting a dying man would all be examples. Care work represents an interesting frontier in the commodification of labor. Historically, it was the responsibility of the kin group to take care of its members in time of need. But multiple factors increased the demand for such services, including increases in life expectancy, the expansion of universal health coverage (with the United States a notable exception among rich countries), and the legal codification of childhood and retirement (discussed in the previous chapter). At the same time, changing patterns of family life – smaller family sizes, the movement of women into the labor force, and changing cultural norms – have decreased the supply of informal and unpaid care work. The end result has been a new conception of care as a commodity (Lopez 2006).

New forms of service employment also entail selling one's appearance, a phenomenon known as aesthetic labor. The term may invoke images of glamorous fashion models traversing the catwalk, and the fashion industry does represent a site of extreme beauty commodification (Mears 2011). But the general idea of selling beauty has disseminated across a range of industries. This is surely the result of two trends unique to advanced capitalism. First is the rise of the field of marketing, which scientifically studies methods for making products appealing to consumers. Firms may take advantage of our innate bias toward physically attractive people (Hamermesh 2011) by requiring someone such as a retail salesperson to dress and act according to particular aesthetic principles (Williams and Connell 2010). Second is the rise of what has been called an "experience economy" (Pine and Gilmore 1999). Rather than enter a space (such as a car dealership) in order to buy something (a car), consumers buy something (such as a cocktail) in order simply to occupy a certain space (a hip new lounge). The physical good itself is secondary to the larger experience of seeing and being seen there. In turn, the workers who staff such places are chosen not because of their technical competence but because they project a certain "look."

To conclude this section, we consider a third form of paid labor, what we can call knowledge work. Examples would include coders, transcriptionists, translators, copyeditors, and others who produce neither physical goods nor emotional states. They are neither managers (indeed, their work is often intensely monitored) nor professionals (in the sense of having a monopoly on some valuable and generalizable expertise). In essence, they are selling their ability to manipulate words, numbers, and symbols – especially in the virtual environments enabled by advancements in information technology. Such occupations possess many of the trappings traditionally associated with good jobs: they take place in an office setting, they often require a post-secondary degree, and so on. But in fact, globalization and the internet are rendering this form of labor less and less valuable. Scanners allow paper documents to be digitized while fiber-optic data cables allow them to be sent instantaneously anywhere in the world. As firms divide up knowledge processes and subcontract them out to suppliers worldwide, the pool of available knowledge workers grows and, all else being equal, the worth of knowledge work decreases accordingly.

An Ontology of the Paycheck

We have just seen that the commensuration of labor is converging on the idea that workers provide labor power (as measured by time) of an emotional and mental (as opposed to simply physical) nature. What, though, of the other side of the exchange? What are the possible substances that can be legitimately provided to employees within a capitalist system? It is common to assume that this substance is cash money: one works and in return receives, if not a wad of bills, then a paycheck, deposit slip, or, increasingly, proof of an electronic transfer of funds. But money, a symbolic and generalized medium of exchange, is actually only one of multiple forms that remuneration can take (Zelizer 1997). In this section we consider five others: payment-in-kind, scrip systems, tangible benefits, intangible benefits, and tips.

Money is a symbol, meaning that it has no value in itself but only insofar as it can be converted into something else. It is also generalizable, meaning that the power of money derives from its ability to allow commensuration across a wide range of domains. But employers can remunerate workers in a ready-at-hand, non-monetary substance: payment in kind, which by its nature is tangible (not symbolic) and specific (not generalizable). In basic terms, these systems involve paying workers wholly or partially with the very products that they produce.

In unregulated capitalisms, these systems appear to be common, suggesting that they are not in employees' interests. To see why, we can consider a well-known example: the infamous "tot system" used for many years by white-owned wineries in the Western Cape region of South Africa. Workers, who were black or coloured, would be paid each day not in money but in wine itself. This created multiple problems for them. In order to obtain other needed goods, they had to sell or trade the wine on the informal market, which takes time and energy. It also encouraged the over-consumption of wine by workers and workers' families, leading to endemic alcoholism and its associated social problems. Wine-makers, by contrast, benefited from the tot system. It lowered their wage bill; allowed them to easily dispose of excess or substandard wine; and created a dependent, essentially drugged, workforce.

As trade unions and governments began to regulate the labor exchange, payment-in-kind systems were targeted for elimination. Employment law today almost always prohibits them. Nonetheless, we see in practice that employers continue to offer their products in exchange for workers' labor power. This would not be as explicit as a sack of wine, but rather something such as a discount on the company's products.

Workers, meanwhile, may be in a position where they are highly dependent upon the employer to satisfy their needs and tastes. It is thus not surprising to find that low-wage fast-food workers, who get short meal breaks and are often mired in poverty, must avail themselves of the slightly discounted (if unhealthy) burgers and fries at their work. They may even use their discounts to purchase extra food to take home with them and share with the family (eerily reminiscent of the tot system). In the retail sector, many clothing stores require sales associates to wear their brands on the floor, such that employee discounts are a *de facto* payment-in-kind. As Williams and Connell (2010) document, many employees are aficionados of such brands and will accept a low-wage retail job simply to avail themselves of the clothing discounts.

Similar to payment-in-kind (i.e., firm-specific, tangible remu-neration) is payment via what is often called "scrip." This is a symbolic medium of payment, handed out to workers as vouchers, chips, bills, stamps, tokens, or some other such tender. In contrast to money, however, scrip is a self-contained system of currency good only at facilities provided or approved by the employer. But when and why would remuneration take the form of scrip rather than money? There might simply be a lack of the latter. Especially in the early history of capitalism, it was common for local areas to develop labor markets before exposure to a central system of currency. This explains as well why scrip systems persisted in isolated areas such as rural towns and distant military bases. In the case of the former, we find the origin of the phrase a "company store": it was the only place in town where workers could spend their pay. In the case of the latter, scrip may be a strategy whereby the employer (the government) attempts to prevent its currency from falling into foreign hands when soldiers venture off-base.

Scrip systems can give rise to unintended consequences. It is unlikely that a company store can provide for all the needs and desires of workers; in response there may develop secondary (black) markets in which scrip is exchanged for the wider currency or other goods and services. Also, because the employer is in the position of a monopolist supplier, it is able to inflate prices and will have little incentive to satisfy its customers/employees. Under capitalism, scrip systems represent a contradiction between free markets in labor yet restricted markets in goods. Not surprisingly, they are often bitterly resented by employees and precipitate the formation of labor unions. Governments, too, generally ban them, both out of concern for the exploitation of workers and owing to fears of the usurpation by private parties of the state's right to generate and control the money supply.

Payment-in-kind and scrip systems are non-monetary forms of remuneration on the decline. But others are on the rise. Consider what are called fringe benefits, which consist of various perks, rewards, and bonuses that are associated with a job. What distinguishes them is that they are easily convertible into a quantitative monetary value, but yet are not normally included in the base salary or wage. Consider a publicly traded company that pays its workers 30,000 euros per year but also grants them a certain number of shares in the company's stock. At any given moment, the total value of these shares can be calculated using the current price of the stock on the relevant exchange. But chances are that if you ask employees, "What do you earn?," most will report their base salary and not bother to do the conversion. The same holds for something such as a retirement plan in which the employer matches the employee's monthly contribution. This is obviously money, but, perhaps because it is not easily liquidated, it is not thought of as a direct source of income. Governments may contribute to this impression, by not treating certain fringe benefits as taxable.

There are a variety of reasons why employers would offer a fringe benefit in lieu of additional salary. First, the fact that they are more common in professional and unionized workplaces suggests that they come about when employees possess a high degree of bargaining power. Second, governments may structure policy so that, intentionally or not, employers are encouraged to offer fringe benefits. This seems to be the case with employer-provided health insurance plans in the United States, long one of the few industrialized nations not to provide universal, state-funded health care. Instead, the government allows employers to classify the cost of health care benefits as a non-taxable expense. Third, certain fringe benefits, such as a profit-sharing plan, may serve as a mechanism by which workers are encouraged to work harder and identify with the goals of their employer (the subject of incentive plans will be discussed further in chapter 6). And, fourth, certain fringe benefits may be viewed by a given culture as an entitlement. For instance, labor law in the Philippines, a majority Catholic nation in Southeast Asia, mandates that all workers receive a Christmas bonus equal to one month's pay by December 24 of the year – referred to euphemistically as the "13th month pay"!

Related to the idea of the fringe benefit, but much more difficult to quantify, is what is called a compensating differential. These are intangible rewards that an employer offers in place of a wage increase. They are often observed when workers accept jobs paying less than what we would otherwise expect given their qualifications and the state of the labor market. Consider a new law school graduate who has a strong belief in protecting the environment. She has two job offers. One is with an oil company where she will be representing a known polluter, but will be paid a wage 10 percent greater than the average for new lawyers. The other is with a non-profit organization that does *pro bono* work for local communities that are victimized by oil spills, and pays 10 percent less than the standard salary. How are we to explain the nature of the employment exchange if she accepts the latter offer?

The answer must be that she is receiving *something else* besides monetary remuneration in the exchange. In this case, we can assume this to be a sense of satisfaction that her professional work matches her personal values. According to Boltanski and Chiapello (2005), the social movements of the 1960s and 1970s were instrumental in transforming the expectations of managerial and professional workers that their work has not simply pecuniary, but expressive and even spiritual benefits. These might include a positive corporate culture, flexible work schedules to meet family and personal needs, and a basic belief in the mission of the organization. The counter-argument is that the 1980s, 1990s, and 2000s witnessed a reverse process, with college graduates moving into the financial sector and sacrificing personal growth in the pursuit of making ever-increasing amounts of money. The metaphor of the "winner-take-all" society (Frank and Cook 1996) aptly captures the result of this sort of compensating differential: greater inequality at the society level.

This brings us to one last form of non-pecuniary remuneration, common in the service sector and known colloquially as tips or gratuities. On the surface, these may look like a wage payment. A bartender delivers a drink to a patron in a timely manner, and in turn receives from the patron a bill or a few coins. But there is a key distinction, namely, that the financial exchange occurs *between employee and client* and not between employee and employer. In fact, in some jurisdictions the law allows employers to pay tipped employees less than the minimum wage; after taxes and deductions, a worker may receive no formal pay at all! In such instances, we can say that while the worker provides physical and emotional labor, the employer provides but a license to work as a private entrepreneur on the premises.

Ethnographic studies of tipped employees support this argument. Paules (1991), for instance, studied waitresses by working as one in a New Jersey diner. She found that they exhibited an entrepreneurial mindset, cultivating clients and demanding that management not interfere with their ability to deliver service. Another example comes from Sallaz's (2002) study of casino dealers in the western United States. During the nineteenth and early twentieth centuries, gambling halls would simply rent out table-space each night to dealers, who traveled around as independent artisans. They paid losses out of their own pocket and kept any winnings. As the industry grew and became more business-like, however, casinos had to hire dealers as official employees. But they continued to let dealers act as entrepreneurs, most notably by allowing them to hustle and keep their nightly "tokes." Research on taxi drivers (Davis 1959), hotel workers (Sherman 2007), and doormen (Bearman 2005) further confirms that tipping is a unique system of remuneration insofar as employers provide workers not wages but the freedom to make tips.

Logics of Pricing

A critical economic sociology of labor must account for the underlying logic by which a particular value is assigned to labor, however it is defined. How are there established equivalencies between the work performed and the remuneration provided? The field of economics devotes a great deal of attention to the question of wages. In theory, this should be a matter of establishing an equilibrium between demand and supply: workers decide the lowest, or reservation, wage at which they will accept a job, while employers raise their offers until a clearing price is reached. In reality, however, wages and salaries often seem to be influenced by non-market mechanisms, as in the example discussed above wherein a series of worker suicides provoked a Chinese manufacturing giant to drastically raise pay rates. Let us consider further how market logics interact with social, cultural, and political processes to generate specific conventions of pricing labor.

Of course, logics of pricing will be connected to whether a particular culture understands employment as the sale of potential activity (labor power) versus work accomplished (labor). If the former, then remuneration will be provided in accord with the total amount of time that a person is in the employ of another. It follows that commensuration will here depend on concrete technologies for measuring and tracking time. The image that first comes to mind is that of workers inserting their identity cards into a "time clock" to stamp them with the exact hour and minute of arriving at and leaving work (though workers of today are just as likely to "log in" via computerized personnel management software as they are to "punch in" an actual clock). The logic of time remuneration further gives rise to particular forms of conflict and bargaining. A company, for instance, might require its office employees to set up their workstations (booting up their computers, preparing the needed files for the day, etc.) *before* logging in to their shifts. Employees might then protest that the ten or so minutes that they spend doing so is in effect uncompensated labor, insofar as they are physically in the office and doing the company's bidding.

Such a dispute about time would be less likely in a system where employers remunerate employees in accord with goods or services produced. One example is the "putting out" system, common in manufacturing historically and in less developed countries today. A business simply contracts with agents to supply a given amount of product by a certain date; as long as the terms of the deal are satisfied, payment occurs (Tilly and Tilly 1997). Even once employees are centralized in factories, offices, or retail establishments, they may be remunerated according to piecework – paid for each item produced and regardless of the time taken to make it (Petersen 1992).

Such systems rely less on instruments for measuring time than on those for determining quality. Payment depends on the product meeting certain standards. A typist, for example, might be paid per page of output, given that each page is of an acceptable quality. To determine this, however, the firm will need to have in place a system for checking the texts (or usually a sample thereof) and determining the cause of any typographical errors. Conflict, too, takes patterned forms in systems of remuneration based upon output. On one hand, there will continuously arise the question: what is the value of the goods that workers produce? On the other, that of: what is the minimum acceptable standard of quality below which a good is not accepted by the employer?

Actual work systems are often a hybrid of time-based and output-based remunerative logics. In the manufacturing sector, many firms pay their production workers a standard hourly wage along with bonuses for pieces produced above some quota. This occurs as well in the service sector, as would be the case for retail associates who receive an hourly wage but also earn a commission on each sale for which they are responsible. The information and technology sector today employs many semi-skilled workers, such as telephone-based customer service representatives, who are paid according to both the time they are working and their output (such as the number of calls that they compete at a certain service level). This explains why, despite the obvious differences between blue-collar settings such as factories and white-collar workplaces such as call centers, many have referred to the latter as "digital assembly lines" (Head 2005: 100).

Regardless of their specific mechanisms, all systems of pricing must be able to give a certain, quantitative value to labor at any given moment. Various theories seek to explain how this occurs. One influential perspective holds that in capitalist economies, a downward pressure is continuously applied to wages, driving them to the point of bare subsistence. The logic is simply that businesses compete not only by increasing sales but also by reducing costs. The costs of raw materials, machinery, and other inputs are usually out of employers' control, but labor is a "variable cost," meaning that it can be lowered or raised by the individual employer. Firms will seek to reduce wages, but should they get too low, then the worker will not be able to survive and reproduce. In the aggregate, wages will tend to converge on this bare minimum. Classical economists, such as Ferdinand Lassalle and David Ricardo, referred to this as the "iron law of wages."

This theory is essential to the critical tradition as well. For Marx (1978b [1849]: 124), the "cost required for the maintenance of the worker" is the "wage minimum." Capitalism, over the broad sweep of time, can never raise remuneration much above this minimum because of the privatized, competitive relations among owners of capital. One rebuttal to this theory is that capitalism is a dynamic system constantly generating new industries and products. To attract workers with specialized skills and education, firms have to offer wages above the survival level. Critical scholars counter that capitalists are equally adept at destroying skills as at creating them. Frederick Taylor, an American writing in the early twentieth century, pioneered the managerial "science" of dividing complex crafts up into simple tasks and then distributing them among a great many unskilled workers. As work is deskilled, it is degraded and thus cheapened (Braverman 1974; Stinchcombe 1959). To the extent that capitalism contains this inherent tendency to suppress wages, how do we explain the reality that average wages in most economies *are* above the bare survival level?

The answer, sociologists often argue, may be less about economics than about politics and culture. It is not a logic internal to markets that determines the wage floor, but rather external principles of citizenship, rights, and governance. First, consider that most countries today have a legally mandated "minimum wage," designed to be greater than the wage minimum described by Marx. These policies developed over the course of the twentieth century, and they certainly did *not* result from largesse on the part of employers. Labor unions and social movements struggled to frame minimum wage laws as a human rights matter and to make states enact policies guaranteeing them. And while it is not uncommon to hear an orthodox economist advocate their repeal during periods of high unemployment, it seems unlikely that this will happen.

On the contrary, minimum wage policies are being expanded in several ways. First, this is being done to account for real versus nominal values. Advocates of workers argue that the official minimum wage should be adjusted frequently to reflect changes in the value of a given unit of currency owing to inflation; or, even better, that it should be defined not nominally but rather as a percentage of some general indicator of the true cost of living.

Second, minimum wage policies are being customized to account for local economic conditions within a given region. This can be seen in current movements to create an entirely new principle of remuneration: a "living wage." Advocates argue that federally mandated minimum wage rates do not reflect cost of living differentials across the various regions of a country, and especially between urban and non-urban areas. Sub-federal jurisdictions such as city and state governments are then pressured to pass their own legislation mandating that employers pay a wage that can support an individual or a family in that jurisdiction. This requires not only the political labor of convincing relevant decision-makers to enact the policy, but also the more technical labor of collecting specific information about the cost of food, housing, and other essentials in a given locality (Martin 2001).

Third, the notion of what constitutes a fair minimum wage is currently being disputed across national boundaries. Globalization means that consumers in rich countries are acquiring more and more of their goods and services from employees in poor countries. But owing to vast geographical distances and the complex nature of modern supply chains, many consumers are not aware of the working conditions and salaries of those who make their stuff. A person may purchase a smart-phone from a company based in a European country known for its strong labor protections, without realizing that the actual production of the phone has been sourced to a third party operating in a country where workers are paid below subsistence-level wages or otherwise exploited.

Many argue that under globalization, individual nation-states are incapable of ensuring a fair wage. If one country neglects to set or enforce a standard, accepted principles of state sovereignty prevent other nation-states from directly enforcing such laws. And if they refuse to buy that nation's products, they could be charged with protectionism and suffer sanctions. What other governance mechanisms might come into play? The handful of supra-national agencies that currently oversee world society (such as the United Nations or World Bank) can establish general principles but they lack authority to create and enforce a global labor law. Regional free trade agreements represent another possibility, as member nations can agree to open trade borders subject to certain conditions, including adherence by all signatories to fair labor standards. But so far at least, advocates have been relatively unsuccessful at inducing negotiators to include labor protections in free trade agreements. Evans and Kay (2008), for example, found that environmentalists were much more effective than were trade unions when it came to influencing the writing of the North American Free Trade Agreement.

Into this gulf have stepped multiple actors seeking to innovate new methods for propagating a living wage standard on a global level. What unites them is that rather than relying upon traditional unilateral regulation, these groups deploy novel techniques to generate leverage over employers across multiple fronts. Consider, for instance, the rise of third-party certification of a good's "fair trade" status (Bartley 2003; Seidman 2007). This is in opposition to the principle of "free trade," which we have established to mean that forces of supply and demand alone determine the price of labor. In brief, activists, social movements, and non-profit organizations have sought to encourage employers to adhere to living wage principles (among other social concerns). They do so by creating new procedures by which auditors establish that a firm is behaving in a "socially responsible" manner. Those who do are rewarded with the right to have a stamp placed on their products, while those who refuse to adhere may be publicly branded as "sweatshops" or even demonstrated against in public "shaming" ceremonies (Chun 2010).

One weakness of such approaches to valuing labor is that they may ultimately rely upon consumers as the arbiter of value. Goods labeled "fair trade" or "sweatshop free" – like produce certified as organic or locally grown – tend to be more expensive than those lacking such labels. While some consumers may be willing to pay this premium regardless of the circumstance, many may opt for cheaper alternatives, especially when the economy is in the doldrums. Even so, it appears that, at a global level, these recent attempts to establish non-market criteria for commensurating labor may have succeeded in creating new norms for what constitutes legitimate behavior by multinational firms. Under the broad rubric of "corporate social responsibility," publics of all sorts are demanding that firms move away from the ruthless pursuit of short-term profits that characterized the recent period of "shareholder capitalism" (Fligstein 2001a).

In the final analysis, this may be the reason why Foxconn gave raises to its Chinese workers. The spate of suicides and the public outcry that followed did not alter the underlying dynamics of supply and demand; rather, they forced the firm to adjust its calculus for remunerating labor by yanking it out of a local economy and thrusting it into the spotlight of an emergent global field. The lesson that this case teaches is that there is no universal logic for commensurating work. Market and non-market principles combine and compete with one another in accord with the larger configuration of political forces and cultural meanings. Commensuration, in short, is an embedded process. In the next chapter we will observe similar dynamics at work in the matching of employers and employees within the context of the larger labor market.

5

Making Labor Markets

In order to study the inner workings of the modern gambling industry, Sallaz (2009) trained as a casino dealer and performed covert ethnographic research at several Las Vegas casinos. He found that as much as dice or cards, shampoos and razors were considered by workers to be essential "tools of their trade." A dealer's career is characterized by near-constant mobility across firms. Casinos quickly fall in an out of favor with tourists and gamblers, meaning that employees have to be proactive about cultivating and maintaining connections at other properties (referred to industry parlance as "building your juice") so that they'll be ready when the time is right to switch jobs. There is an additional problem, however. Many (though by no means all) dealers regularly engage in an activity that is considered morally problematic by the larger society: drug use. To maintain alertness during their "graveyard shifts," they consume "uppers" such as amphetamines and cocaine; after work, they consumer "downers" such as marijuana and Valium to decompress and facilitate sleep in the bright desert daylight.

While floor managers generally adopt a "don't ask, don't tell" approach to this behavior, the personnel who staff the casinos' hiring departments do not. Standard corporate policy dictates that all job applicants have clipped from their heads (or occasionally armpits, chest, or legs) a few snippets of hair, the follicles of which are then chemically analyzed for evidence of drug use. To pass this test, drastic measures are required. Some men simply shave their heads (and indeed their entire bodies), in order to then be administered what they refer to as a preferred "piss test" (chemical analysis of urine reveals only the past several weeks of drug use, as opposed to the hair tests, which can evidence use dating back months or even years). Women, along with those men who could not bear to part with their locks, would turn to the internet to procure such products as "Ultra Clean," "Toxin Wash," and "Precision Cleanse": shampoos specially formulated to fool drug tests.

A "labor market" is typically defined in textbooks as a social space in which employers are matched with workers seeking to sell their labor. The term brings to mind an image of fresh graduates submitting their résumés to potential employers, who in turn carefully scan them to see which applicants have the highest amount of "human capital": that is, education, experience, and skills. A job-seeker, meanwhile, systematically evaluates job offers to select the one that best suits her preferences. After this initial matching period is concluded, the new employee embarks upon a career inside the organization. She works "9 to 5," five days each week, and finds that, over the course of her career, her loyalty, seniority, and performance are appropriately rewarded by her employer.

This idealized image of the labor market could not be further from the lived experience of casino service workers, which consists of building juice, hopping jobs, and scrubbing hair. But in many ways it is the insecure yet entrepreneurial croupier, more so than the staid "organization man," who best exemplifies where capitalism is headed. Across advanced economies, firms are increasingly reluctant to give permanent contracts to employees, or even to hire employees at all as opposed to contracting for temporary or outsourced labor. As a result, even educated and skilled workers must constantly keep one eye on the larger job market and be ready to jump back into it at a moment's notice. They must monitor their personal appearance, maintain their professional networks, and, should they become unemployed, attend seminars to learn the powers of positive thinking (Sharone 2007).

This chapter argues that at the same time that the employment relationship becomes impersonal and commoditized, the search-strategies of both firms and workers remain deeply embedded in the social. First, buyers and sellers of labor are flesh-and-blood people whose actions are guided by cultural conventions and moral convictions. Second, their decisions are often influenced by cognitive biases and information constraints. And, third, hiring processes take place within the context of organizational structures (such as personal networks) and regulatory institutions (such as anti-discrimination law). To illuminate the embeddedness of labor markets, we will systematically consider the matching process from the perspective of employers and employees. In addition, we draw attention to emergent technologies and practices by which each party presents itself to and evaluates the other.

Looking for Labor

Prior to the great transformation, those who possessed capital could procure labor in a variety of ways, from familial obligation to charismatic persuasion to coercive enslavement. As we elaborated in the previous two chapters, modern capitalism narrows the range of legitimate mechanisms for procuring labor to one: the purchase of commodified labor from a legally bounded labor market. This raises a series of interesting questions concerning the strategies of those who are buyers in this market (i.e., employers). What are the trade-offs that must be made between finding a perfect worker and finding an acceptable one in an adequate time frame and at a reasonable cost? How, over time, have states moved to regulate the hiring process, and in line with what principles of governance? Are there circumstances in which a firm may opt to not hire an employee at all, but rather contract with a third party to provide the good or service? These are the questions addressed in this section.

The sociologist Max Weber postulated that capitalism advances hand in hand with rationalization. Once market society has been broadly legitimated, pressures of competition narrow the range of viable organizational forms to those that embody maximally efficient practices and procedures. Regarding the acquisition of staff, a bureaucracy (which Weber took to be the ideal type of the instrumentally rational organization) will collect as much information as possible on candidates. It will subject them to various exams and require from them qualifications that match precisely the forms of work they are to perform.

Today, we find that modern technology offers employers myriad methods for looking deep into the hearts and minds of potential employees. Reading résumés, checking references, and conducting interviews continue to be essential tools in the bureaucratic evaluation process. But technologies are now available of which Weber could not have dreamt. Technical exams can gauge very specific skill-sets (such as a receptionist's typing speed or an athlete's vertical leap), while psychological testing can generate detailed personality profiles (such as how extroverted or insecure one is). Chemical analysis of urine and hair cells, like that in the tests routinely administered to casino workers, can reveal whether an applicant has used drugs and alcohol well into the distant past. It is even now possible to take a saliva sample and analyze an individual's genetic makeup, such as whether one is susceptible to particular diseases or mental disorders.

Contra Weber's assumptions, the vast majority of employers do not utilize the full range of screening technologies available to them. This is due to two reasons. First, information itself is not free (Akerlof 1970; Arrow 1966; Solow 1990). It would be quite expensive for a firm to have its human resources department perform every single test that is now technically possible. Furthermore, many of these methods for collecting information on applicants have themselves become commodities. If a form of testing has been patented, a firm will have to pay a fee to a specialized agency to administer it and interpret its results. For most firms, it is not worth the cost to thoroughly research every candidate for every position. Decisions must be made as to which testing procedures are appropriate for various types of personnel. Second, no predictive mechanism can be 100 percent accurate. An engineering graduate with perfect grades may fail to innovate new ideas for the technology firm that hires her; while a college dropout like Steve Jobs, overlooked by potential employers, may go on to start his own company and revolutionize the computing business.

Given these constraints, we should not be surprised to find that actual hiring processes veer from the bureaucratic procedures described by Weber. In fact, a great deal of research reveals that managers, rather than maximize the amount of information available to them, seek to reduce it. They simplify their complex environments by organizing data into manageable chunks and analyzing them through basic heuristics, schemata, signals, and frames (Kahneman 2011; Spence 1973). The existence of such "bounded rationality," as Simon (1997b) termed it, illuminates the multiple ways in which labor markets remain embedded in the social.

This holds not simply for low-skilled and entry-level jobs but even for the highest echelons of corporate governance. For instance, Khurana (2002) documented how large firms go about choosing new chief executive officers (CEOs). One might assume that, given their immense resources, corporate boards would be pioneering the use of evidence-based hiring processes (Bebchuk and Fried 2004). Executives with strong track records would be rewarded with better positions, while those with a history of failure would be forced out of the job market. But in fact, executive search committees are easily swept up in ephemeral fads and appear to fall irrationally for charismatic figures who have been hyped up in the business press. This sets in motion an unhealthy dynamic in which firms hire CEOs with the wrong backgrounds, who then underperform on the job and are fired, leading the whole process to commence again.

Of course, the perpetuation of such "irrational" customs means that some firms can gain a competitive advantage by innovating and rationalizing their hiring practices. This was the case in professional baseball during the 1990s, as documented by Lewis (2003) in the book *Moneyball*. Throughout the twentieth century, baseball teams had relied on veteran scouts to choose players in free agency and in the amateur draft. Like corporate boards, scouts felt they could intrinsically recognize future stars through an eyeball test.

This led to the selection of charismatic young players with "confident swaggers" and "pretty swings," but who all too often failed
to perform. Several small-market teams, however, used statistics to
develop new measurements of a player's value to a team. Rather
than paying millions of dollars to brawny batsmen who occasionally hit awe-inspiring homeruns, clubs such as the Oakland
Athletics overachieved by paying mere thousands for portly fielders
with the knack for getting on base and tiring out pitchers.

Further examples demonstrate that employers' strategies for
finding workers are embedded within longstanding conventions
for managing information. In many countries, a key aspect of job
screening is the perusal of résumés on which applicants have been
taught to comprehensively list their accomplishments and qualifications. For personnel officers, this can produce the sensation of
suffocating under a mountain of paper (or, increasingly, text files
such as PDFs and Microsoft Word documents). In response, they
develop shortcuts for quickly scanning the résumés in order to
identify characteristics they deem to be pertinent. This practical
response to information overload is neither perfectly rational nor
purely idiosyncratic, but rather represents the confluence of multiple social processes. Rivera (2011) thus found that hiring agents
at Wall Street firms routinely discard résumés from applicants
lacking a degree from a top-tier Ivy League school, while following up on the résumés of those who excelled in upper-middle-class
sports such as lacrosse and crew. These markers are taken to
signify that the applicant has intelligence and class, yet is not a
nerd or bore.

The labor market for white-collar workers operates quite
differently in Japan (Gerlach 1997). Rather than continuously
reviewing résumés as positions become open, firms conduct
a single recruitment drive every spring to hire college seniors
for lifelong positions. This is quite consequential for the latter
because, according to custom, if one is not hired at this stage,
one is condemned to a career of low wages and low social status.
It explains as well why Japanese students are underrepresented
among international scholars: study abroad entails missing out on
the annual rite of passage back home. For firms, the strategy is not

to hire people with specialized skills but rather to select those who exhibit a general aptitude to learn and fit in with the existing corporate culture. Concretely, this personnel regime means that new hires tend to look like the existing managerial hierarchy in terms of gender and class background (Aoki et al. 2007).

It is difficult to say whether the American or the Japanese system is a more efficient way to procure personnel. At different points in the twentieth century each was considered a paragon for corporate governance, while the sluggish performance of the American and Japanese economies in the early twenty-first has cast doubt upon both systems. However, it should be apparent that in each case, entrenched conventions of hiring rely upon homophily, a term sociologists use to refer to what appears to be a natural human desire to surround ourselves with others who resemble us. In a historical perspective, homophily appears not as some social pathology but as the default way to find people to do important work for you – enlisting your friends, kin, co-ethnics, and so on, was simply the norm. But, when applied to capitalist labor markets, it produces outcomes that are deemed to be inappropriate, inefficient, and even immoral. Most notably, homophily becomes synonymous with what is known as discrimination, a phenomenon assumed to generate and perpetuate social divisions – what Tilly (1999) calls "durable inequality." As such, it has become the target of one of the major global social movements of the past fifty years.

States Step In

Because it is timely and costly to collect information on all potential employees, employers often use various shortcuts and heuristics during the recruitment process. Two in particular – nepotism and stereotyping – are increasingly proscribed by modern states seeking to enforce principles of equity and justice.

The word "nepotism" comes from a Latin word meaning nephew. We thus say that a hiring practice is nepotistic if favoritism is accorded to members of one's own family or clan.

Stereotyping, in turn, means that you make judgments about an individual based upon his or her membership in some larger social category. An employer who refused to consider Catholic job applicants because he believed they were lazy would be engaging in stereotyping. Both practices rely upon distinguishing between in-group and out-group members in a way that favors the former and discriminates against the latter. And both seemingly offer advantages to employers. When you hire a family member, for instance, you presumably get an employee whom you already know and trust. And stereotyping allows you to boil a complex process down to a simple one: X people are good while Y people are bad, so I will hire only X people (Arrow 1998; Stryker 2001).

Prior to the advent of modern capitalism, nepotism and stereotyping were the default strategies for finding workers. Feudalism, slave economies, and caste-based societies were all ones in which your status at birth determined your eventual occupation. Even in industrialized market economies today, we find many small and family-owned businesses wherein managers exhibit a "traditional habitus" (Sallaz 2009): that is, a way of seeing the world that relies on common sense and distrusts bureaucratic procedure.

Traditional hiring practices, however, are not without flaw. Nepotism may backfire as family members prove to be untrustworthy and incompetent, while stereotypes may be based on biases and mistaken beliefs. Employers who use these strategies will presumably find themselves at a disadvantage relative to competitors who evaluate applicants based on more objective criteria. For this reason, many economists, echoing Weber, postulate that discriminatory labor market practices will eventually be eliminated by competitive market forces (Becker 1971). More generally, nepotism and stereotyping, because they conflict with the values of democratic society, have become targets of governments who attempt to regulate them out of existence.

The twentieth century witnessed what we may call a "minority rights revolution," as various disempowered and disenfranchised groups were granted protection from discrimination in the labor market (Skrentny 2002). One thrust for such protections derived from mobilizations on the part of local peoples of the global South against colonial rule by European and North American powers. From India to Indonesia to South Africa, colonialism had been synonymous with the exclusion of "locals" from skilled occupations and positions of authority. When colonial regimes fell and the previously marginalized came to power, states often (though not always) instituted proactive policies to increase their representation in key sectors of the economy such as within government and at the top rungs of firms (Burawoy 1972). Entrenched managers often protested what they viewed as an infusion of unqualified personnel, but in such historically significant circumstances social concerns readily trumped economic ones.

Relatedly, many democratic countries in the developed world experienced mass mobilization by disadvantaged and economically frustrated minorities. In the United States during the 1960s and 1970s, this took the form of the civil rights movement, spearheaded by such inspirational leaders as Martin Luther King Jr. and Cesar Chavez. The apogee of this movement was the passage by the US Congress in 1964 of Title VII of the Civil Rights Act. It pronounced that:

> It shall be an unlawful employment practice for an employer . . . to fail or refuse to hire or to discharge any individual, or otherwise to discriminate against any individual with respect to his compensation, terms, conditions, or privileges of employment, because of such individual's race, color, religion, sex, or national origin. (SEC. 2000e-2. [Section 703])

In the decades to follow, many nations adopted similar legislation and created independent agencies to enforce it. We can say that the anti-discrimination zeitgeist truly went global.

Three issues define the current economic-sociological research program in regard to employer discrimination. First is the issue of how and why certain social statuses, but not others, come to be defined as "protected categories." In his historical study, Skrentny (1996) found that US law protects some racial and ethnic groups who mobilized for their rights, such as African Americans and Latinos, but not others, such as Jewish Americans or Irish Americans. Some groups, such as Asian Americans and Native

Americans, were automatically included in anti-discrimination law because they had in recent decades come to be thought of as discrete "minorities." Other countries, to the extent that their systems of racial classification vary, legislate discrimination issues differently. In France, for instance, the state does not classify citizens as members of particular racial groups, meaning that advocates of labor market regulation must find other ways to protect minorities from discrimination. And in Brazil, racial categories are fluid and constantly evolving, meaning that the state has to evaluate claims of discrimination and devise redress in a contextual way (Telles 2004).

The second issue studied by economic sociologists is that of how discrimination laws are enacted in practice. Research frequently uncovers surprising dynamics that illustrate how economic processes are embedded in larger political institutions. Consider the case of the United States. Following the passage of the 1964 Civil Rights Act, the actual efficacy of anti-discrimination law was dampened down by both Congress, which underfunded the main enforcement body (the Equal Employment Opportunity Commission), and the courts, which over time altered the definition of discrimination to include only the most egregious of acts. It was only through the efforts of dedicated lawyers, union officials (Pedriana and Stryker 2004), and human resource officials (Dobbin 2011) that states and large firms came to take the inherent value of "diversity" for granted and to institute organization practices to support it.

Documenting forms of discrimination that are not covered by existing law is a third frontier of research. Pager (2009), for instance, finds that employers are unlikely to consider the job applications of those who possess a criminal record, even for entry-level and low-skill positions, presumably because they interpret such biographical information as evidence of more general character flaws. Gays and lesbians constitute other groups that are often negatively stereotyped by mainstream culture, and are less likely to be protected by employment law. But as Raeburn (2004) documents, gay and lesbian professionals have successfully mobilized to pressure large corporations to institute gay-inclusive policies. As should be clear by these examples, employers within systems of regulated capitalism have a great many factors to consider when evaluating potential workers. Given such complications, one might wonder under what conditions it makes sense for employers to "purchase" workers at all. Are there other mechanisms for acquiring labor? If so, what are they and how do firms decide among them?

Buy, Make, or Outsource?

It is often assumed that a defining characteristic of capitalism is the alchemy by which it transforms a vast mass of human beings into commodities that can be purchased by employers. The end result of this process we call a society-wide, or external, labor market. But in fact there are other ways that firms can organize labor for the production of their goods and services. One is to rely on the external labor market only rarely, instead creating the appropriate labor supply institutions inside of the firm's own boundaries. Another is to cease making goods or services entirely, instead purchasing them from some external supplier which itself hires the employees to do the work. The general historical movement appears to be from the former, known as building an internal labor market, to the latter, known as outsourcing.

Suppose a firm needs employees. A handful of veteran workers have retired, or new orders are coming in and production must be increased. Instead of placing job advertisements publicly, the firm could fill the positions from within, for instance by promoting or retraining current employees. To the extent that this becomes standard practice, we speak of the existence of an internal labor market. It is still considered a market, because we have a buyer (the firm) of a commodity (labor); but it is internal because the supply pool is restricted to current organizational members, who are already familiarized with corporate culture and policies. At the extreme, firms may even establish their own training institutions, such as apprenticeship programs or vocational schools, to secure a dedicated supply of labor. Under such conditions, firms are producing workers at the same time that they are producing goods and services.

Like nepotism or stereotyping, an internal labor market can be seen as a solution to the problem of transaction costs (Williamson 1998). Finding and evaluating potential workers requires time and resources. They are also processes plagued by uncertainty and a dependence on external institutions: what if a certain number of workers with a certain skill-set are needed, but the larger labor market can't provide them? By generating their own pipeline of talent, firms with an internal labor market buffer themselves against potential shortages and ensure themselves a steady supply of labor. Not surprisingly, internal labor markets are considered appropriate for conditions in which employers will prioritize long-term stability, employee loyalty, and firm-specific expertise.

A prime example is a state's military apparatus. Because it is largely immune from short-term fluctuations in demand for its services (most countries do not gut their militaries next year because of a lack of war this year), it requires a large body of "workers" who are ready to be deployed on short notice – hence the term "standing army." It possesses a monopoly on its product – that is, the expertise to wage mass warfare – meaning that most needed skills (such as machine gun operation) are not taught in the general education system. Loyalty to the organization is encouraged by rewarding seniority and penalizing premature departures. Except for recruiting, just about all personnel allocation within a military bureaucracy takes the form of internal movement of a lateral or vertical sort.

Private sector firms can also use internal labor markets. In the advanced industrial economies of the twentieth century, this complex mode of regulating labor transactions was labeled simply "Fordism." This referred to the fact that for large manufacturers operating under conditions of minimal competition and mass production, it made a great deal of sense to have a large and stable workforce. (Hence the reason why these workforces were known as "industrial armies.") Employees were granted job security and possessed many rights, often spelled out explicitly in collective bargaining agreements and corporate procedure manuals. As reported by ethnographers (Burawoy 1979a), workers in Fordist companies eventually came to think of themselves not as commodities purchased on a market, but as citizens of a company-state.

This all does not mean that militaries and car companies can only be organized as internal labor markets. Britain contracted German soldiers, known as Hessians, to fight the American Revolutionary War, while the American military relied heavily on private contractors to wage the Second Gulf War in Iraq. In recent decades, the Ford Motor Corporation has shifted from building its own auto components to acquiring them from global suppliers. The use of internal versus external labor markets is not a strict binary but rather a continuum of practices. And over the past several decades, entirely new options have emerged as more and more organizations have opted to not hire workers at all. Instead, they buy from some outside entity the goods that they previously had made themselves, "in-house." They opt, that is, to outsource. Because it represents a radical departure from the previous era in which firms relied on labor markets, the emergent system is often referred to as post-Fordism (Sabel and Zeitlin 1985).

Outsourcing to a third party offers some obvious advantages. To the extent that work is displaced to a region where wages are lower (and all else being equal), the overall cost of production is reduced as well. This is what most people envision when they hear the term "outsourcing": a textile factory closing in New York and opening in Vietnam, a technology firm laying off engineers and hiring temps, or a call center being relocated from London to Bangalore, all in order to save money. But the post-Fordist firm also achieves greater flexibility (and at the same time that the post-Fordist worker experiences greater risk and insecurity). Rather than hire employees with a guarantee (explicit or otherwise) of job security, firms can negotiate short-term contracts with various suppliers. This is very much the business model of the largest company in the world today – Walmart – which excels in coordinating global supply chains: that is, in moving cheap goods from Chinese factories to American retail establishments (Lichtenstein 2009).

But outsourcing rather than hiring labor directly has disadvantages for employers. Most fundamentally, they risk losing familiarity with the production process itself. This may be a tolerable risk if the particular input is not related to the firm's core competency (as when an auto plant outsources its janitorial services), but the firm risks eroding knowledge and control over the production process if it contracts for too many inputs (as when said plant outsources the manufacture of its brake components). Where exactly a firm draws the line around its core competencies will depend on multiple factors, not all of them reducible to explicit economic calculation. For instance, as developed economies have experienced economic malaise, more and more blame has been placed on firms that engage in outsourcing, especially to foreign locales. Publics accuse them of being unpatriotic, while politicians consider measures that would punish those that engage in outsourcing and offshoring (Phillips 2010). The tide of history suggests, however, that such restrictions will meet with limited success.

Labor for Sale

Thus far we have examined labor markets from the perspective of potential purchasers of labor. Employers' strategies for finding workers are strategic and patterned, drawing as they do upon heuristics, networks, and conventions (and even in the face of shifting regulatory environments). As we turn our attention to the other party to the exchange – employment-seekers – we find the same principle to hold. They, too, find and evaluate exchange partners in line with simplifying heuristics and with the help of networks of family, friends, and kin. And they, too, have been affected by the recent transformation from Fordist internal labor markets to post-Fordist contracting. The strategies by which sellers of labor find buyers, in short, are embedded in social, political, and cultural frameworks.

Émile Durkheim (1997 [1893]: 311) argued that a well-functioning society establishes channels through which each person can find an occupation matching his or her "abilities and tastes." In a capitalist economy, every job will require certain abilities. This holds not only for high-skilled positions (such as a surgeon, for which a medical degree and extensive training are required) but even those that are commonly labeled low-skilled or unskilled (a fast-food worker, for instance, must be able to understand the local language and perform basic calculations). Insofar as these abilities are not natural, but the product of socialization and education, people will enter the labor market at different points in their life cycle and with variable amounts of leverage. Combine this with the fact that individuals will have different values and interests, along with varying opportunities and motivations for finding work, and we begin to see how complex is any given society's "supply" of labor.

Sociological research has demonstrated that people find jobs in line with logics and strategies that reflect their position in various non-economic environs. First off, employment-seekers are not perfectly liquid commodities; they tend to be *spatially embedded.* They exhibit, that is, a certain degree of connectedness to their current place of residence, which in turn influences how willing they are to relocate to accept a job offer in an alternate locale. This can be seen whenever working parents turn down promotions that would entail transferring to another city; they may place greater value on making sure that their children do not have to switch schools or adjust to a new neighborhood.

The mobility of labor is also affected by the characteristics of a country's housing system. Consider the mixture of rented versus owner-occupied housing. Workers who rent their dwellings can more easily pull up stakes and relocate in response to changing economic conditions, while homeowners are constrained in that they must first sell or rent out their homes. This difference is exacerbated during recessions, when home values decline at the same time that the unemployment rate rises. States that encourage home-ownership through measures such as tax breaks for mortgage interest thus unintentionally restrict the mobility of labor (Moretti 2012).

Even when people do relocate in search of work, their mobility patterns are influenced by their existing social relations. This is true even of those who migrate to new countries. Research establishes that international migrants typically move not haphazardly but to places where members of their kin network have already established roots. The latter have started businesses, acquired a foothold in local industries, and sent home information about job opportunities (Light 1984; Waldinger and Lichter 2003).

States play a role in the migration process. Many developed countries have seen fertility rates drop dramatically over the past century, often to below the replacement rate (i.e., the number of births needed to keep the overall population steady). In response, governments have adopted a range of positions in regard to the immigration issue. Some, such as Canada, actively encourage immigration and promote multiculturalism (Bloemraad 2006); some, such as the United States, restrict immigration to a few favored groups but otherwise guard their borders fastidiously; while others, such as Japan, are unequivocally hostile to immigrants and even offer them monetary payments to repatriate (Tabuchi 2009). On the flip side, "sending states" have a range of options as well. They can seek to prevent citizens from going abroad as workers, especially when they possess education and valued skills (a phenomenon known as brain drain); or they can actively encourage and even facilitate migration, to the point that their national economies become heavily dependent upon the remittances that overseas workers provide (Rodriguez 2010).

As migration illustrates, the strategies of job-seekers exhibit *network embeddedness*. Just as employers may prefer to engage in nepotism rather than evaluate every single applicant within the larger labor market, so, too, may workers find it expeditious to procure employment through referrals, "word of mouth," and recommendations. This is one of the key findings of a classic study by Granovetter (1995 [1974]). The professional workers whom he interviewed had found their jobs not through formal channels (such as public advertisements), but through information gleaned from personal contacts. Notably, these contacts were typically people with whom they had only modest familiarity. It is not your spouse or best friend who alerts you to job openings (because you are so close them, your knowledge is likely to overlap anyway), but an old pal from school or a distant uncle (who are likely to have access to information that you don't). This particular form of network embeddedness has been designated the "strength of weak ties" (Granovetter 1973).

Of course, individuals vary in terms of the number and quality of personal connections that they possess. Real-world labor markets are thus stratified not only by the objective qualifications of prospective employees, but also by these individuals' "social capital" (Portes 2010). This can generate disadvantage for women, who are expected to spend their free time doing household labor and childcare rather than socializing and cultivating professional connections (Roth 2006). And it can have perverse consequences for ethnic minorities and the poor. In an intriguing study, Smith (2005) found that poor African-American workers in Chicago were reluctant to convey information about job-opportunities to their relations. The concern was that the latter would perform poorly or otherwise embarrass the former. As one informant in the study advised her friends applying for work in her company: "Don't put my name on it [i.e., the job application]" (Smith 2005: 1).

There is a third way in which the strategies of job-seekers depart from a basic model of commodity exchange. People are reflexively aware that they possess a subjective value that does not directly reflect their objective qualifications, or human capital. We can refer to this as their *biographical embeddedness*. As we saw earlier, employers appear to have a natural tendency to evaluate applicants through the use of stereotypes, even if these are both fallacious and increasingly deemed illegal. But job-seekers are not dupes, and they are surely aware if and when they possess some characteristic that would disadvantage them in the eyes of evaluators. The sociologist Erving Goffman (1963) defined such characteristics as stigmas, and he documented a variety of ways in which people can manage them when interacting with "normals." It is in this sense that aspirant employees are best conceptualized as strategic social actors rather than inert commodities.

An unfortunate example is the pressure felt by job applicants from minority ethnic groups to dissemble their identities. Many

African-American professionals, for example, report "whitening" their résumés by leaving out participation in advocacy groups for minorities and even going so far as to change their names – as when Tahani Tompkins, a recent college graduate in Chicago, signed her résumé as T. S. Tompkins (Luo 2009). Further, once hired, minority employees feel pressured to refrain from advocating for their rights lest they be accused of rocking the boat (Kanter 1993 [1977]).

Of course, a fine line separates skillful impression management from unlawful misrepresentation. It is likely a good idea to wear a long-sleeved shirt to your job interview if you have extensive arm tattoos; telling the interviewer that you graduated from a prestigious college, when in fact you didn't finish secondary school, is not. The larger lesson is that job-seekers have at their disposal a variety of licit and semi-licit tactics for covering up or diverting attention from aspects of the self that might constitute stigmata in an employer's eyes.

There is one final way in which the labor market can be said to be biographically embedded. Because of their early experiences, people internalize a certain image of themselves and their proper place in the world. Members of symbolically denigrated groups (such as ethnic minorities, women, homosexuals, or the poor) will have an innate sense of the forms of work and rewards that are appropriate for "people like us." Under the right circumstances, this sense of exclusion can lead to activism, mobilization, and even revolution. But more routinely, it generates and reinforces what the sociologist Bourdieu (2001) refers to as "symbolic violence": that is, the largely hidden mechanisms by which people's deep-seated dispositions constrain their life chances independent of any immediate external constraint. It is symbolic violence that discourages an otherwise qualified applicant with a strong regional speech accent from applying for a professional job in a large urban center. It may also explain why women are less forceful and more pliant than men when negotiating salaries with employers (Bowles and McGinn 2008). The concept of symbolic violence demonstrates the unique status of human labor: this is an embodied and reflexive commodity that cannot be adequately analyzed except in terms of its position within larger spatial, network, and biographical configurations.

Toward Continuous Commodification

Earlier we introduced post-Fordism, the epochal shift whereby firms increasingly eschew internal labor markets in favor of various outsourced work arrangements. But how has this shift affected the lives of workers and job-seekers? On a fundamental level, it has rewritten the implicit terms of the exchange between employers and employees. The former are increasingly unlikely to offer job security or even formal employment status. As a result, it becomes more and more difficult to secure a "good job" (Kalleberg 2009) that provides a stable career within the boundaries of a single organization (Aubenas 2011).

Across all industries and fields, employees have to think about more than just performing well and advancing in their current jobs. At any time, their tenure with their current employer could end and they could find themselves thrust back onto the labor market. Life is characterized not by security and stability, but by a "continuous commodification." This has a variety of implications. It means that employees should be concerned with keeping their skills and knowledge up to date. To the extent that they are repeatedly put into competition with others, they must be willing to work harder and for lower wages. It will be more difficult for them to plan ahead and put down roots. And above all else, they must be flexible and willing to tolerate risk. As Smith (2001: 7) argues: "[U]ncertainty and unpredictability, and to varying degrees personal risk, have diffused into a broad range of postindustrial workplaces, services and production alike."

Of course, in the early stages of capitalism, before states and labor unions pressed to regulate the employment exchange, a typical life entailed a constant search for wage labor. In his study of the nineteenth-century factory system, Jacoby (2004 [1985]) described how skilled craftpersons had to congregate at factory gates each morning and wait for foremen to throw apples into the crowd. Those lucky enough to catch an apple were hired for the day, while the rest had to wait and try again the following morning. The international union movement of the nineteenth and twentieth centuries was in large part a reaction to such arbitrary governance of the labor market and the insecurity it imposed upon workers.

Even in regulated capitalisms, there are ranges of occupations that entail constant (daily or even hourly) search for short-term employment contracts. For some of these workers, the ephemeral nature of their craft represents not a source of shame but a badge of honor. Consider performers and artists, whose employment histories may consist of no permanent affiliations but rather a long string of "gigs" of varying duration. Despite such insecurity, their lives retain a romantic allure to many of those who are "tied down" by permanent employment and who yearn for the freedom of a rock star's or beatnik novelist's life "on the road."

Closely associated with images of freedom are those of the strong, independent (and often masculine) freelancer. In an ethnographic study of *esquineros* – male, Spanish-speaking day laborers – Purser (2009) documented a precarious existence in which aspirant workers gather early every morning on a street corner to auction themselves off to prospective employers in passing cars. This is the epitome of a spot market in which human beings are commodified! Yet rather than bemoan their existence, the *esquineros* took pride in the fact they were not being forced into a nearby and "regulated" employment center. As one stated: "[The center] is full of lazy people with problems. Here on the street are all of the healthy, strong, and hard-working men. I would be ashamed or embarrassed to be [one of them]. . . . They are fucking weaklings." A similar dynamic was found in a recent study of forest-fire fighters, who equated contingent and seasonal employment with toughness and authenticity (Desmond 2009). Both cases illustrate how the meaning of any labor market situation ultimately depends on its moral valence for participants.

The interplay of post-Fordist corporate restructuring and employee meaning-making can be seen clearly in the recent growth of a "temp economy" across many professional and white-collar settings (Hatton 2011). In generations past, a high percentage of college-educated job-seekers would have been directly offered secure employment in established firms. Increasingly, however, they find no other point of entry into their desired fields than through the myriad staffing agencies that specialize in providing firms with labor on a temporary basis. As early as the 1970s, Gannon (1974) documented a quirky "London agency [that] operates a bus, equipped with telephone, radio and portable type-writers, that cruises the financial district and drops off workers at a moment's notice."

Today, temporary help services (THS) represent a multi-billion dollar industry. In the United States alone, the number of THS agencies grew from 800 in 1960 to 40,000 in 2009 (Smith and Neuwirth 2009). Nor do THS agencies simply provide stopgap employment for people before they obtain their "dream jobs." The phrase "permatemp" has been coined to describe those who desire steady employment, but who remain stuck in the purgatory that is temp work for months and even years.

For employees, temp work shrouds a key aspect of the larger employment exchange. Yes, insofar as a paycheck is issued to them each week, it seems obvious that they are commodifying and selling their labor. But who is purchasing it? Is it the THS agency that originally sent them out to their jobs? Or is it the company to which they report each day and that often requires them to wear its uniforms and speak its scripts? In a study of "CompTech," a technology firm that relies heavily on temporary contracts, Smith (1998: 420) described the "fractured world of the temporary worker," some of whom "were unable to specify who their employer was." Furthermore, many were shunned or treated poorly by CompTech's (increasingly shrinking pool of) permanent employees.

Another way to analyze temp work is as an exchange of labor that remains perpetually in a trial phase. Employees have made known their intent to sell themselves by registering with a THS firm and agreeing to a short-term contract. Potential buyers in turn receive this labor at a discounted price (insofar as temp workers on average receive lower total remuneration than do permanent workers) and with minimal commitment to eventually complete the exchange. While some workers may find this situation to be beneficial (as would a student seeking summer employment), on the whole it would seem to benefit buyers of labor. The research findings of Gottfried (1991) support this contention. They describe how constant anxiety over one's job status produces a powerful disciplinary effect, as workers worry that any absences or miscues will ruin their chances of obtaining a permanent "gig" with the firm (or even of receiving better short-term gigs from the THS agency).

As the example of temp work illustrates, modes of labor exchange bleed into modes of labor control. Common sense holds that people respond to incentives. Thus, tantalizing workers with "carrots" such as permanent positions or promotions would seem to be an effective mechanism by which firms induce them to work harder – as would threatening them with "sticks" of dismissal or the withholding of future work assignments. But are incentives the primary way through which employers elicit effort from their employees? Or are other mechanisms of control at work? In the following chapter we explore such questions.

6

Controlling Labor

Frederick Taylor, the American engineer who in the early twentieth century devised a devilishly ingenious system of management that to this day bears his name, claimed to have drawn inspiration after noticing a contrast in the behavior of his employees. On Monday mornings, they sauntered into the workplace and moved slowly all day long. If one man picked up the pace, his co-workers would cast him deadly stares until he got the message and slowed down. Yet just the day before, Taylor had observed these same men in the local parks playing their hearts out at various sporting events. They ran as fast as they could, covered in sweat, and if one man slowed the pace he would be derided by his teammates. Taylor (1913) took two lessons from these observations. The first was that the workers were not inherently lazy. Rather, they were engaging in a conscious and collective effort to withhold effort, an industrial pathology that he diagnosed as "systematic soldiering." Second, he deduced that this disease could be remedied via the application of scientific principles. Managers, in this view, can design work systems to make sure that every employee works as hard as possible.

By now, Taylorism has been in practice for over a century. It has been implemented in countless workplaces; it has been refined and tinkered with; and in many cases it has been supplanted by entirely new philosophies of management. But the underlying "pathology" remains uncured. In workplaces of all sorts, a battle continues to rage between supervisors who urge their employees to do more and workers who would rather do less.

For scholars writing in the Marxist tradition, this is not at all surprising. Insofar as capitalism estranges us from our species being and exploits us by paying us less than we deserve, it makes perfect sense that workers will conspire to soldier, slow down, and otherwise slack off. Once circumstances become bad enough, Marx predicted, workers will engage in more unified and strenuous collective action, ranging from strikes to political movements (a topic to be explored in the following chapter). But one need not be a full-fledged Trotskyite to recognize that the interests of employers and employees are often (if not always) incompletely aligned. The former desire high-quality work delivered as quickly as possible; the latter desire to be recognized as human beings and not merely machines. The former want profits for the firm; the latter want meaningful work, good pay, and basic dignity (Hodson 2001).

The field of economics has historically neglected the question of labor control. As Ronald Coase (1992: 714) stated in his 1991 Nobel Prize lecture: "What happens in between the purchase of the factors of production and the sale of the goods that are produced by these factors is largely ignored [by economists]." In recent decades, labor control has been discussed as a principal–agent problem analyzable as an issue of contract enforcement. How does an employer (principal) make sure an employee (agent) lives up to the terms of the job contract? How does the former make sure the latter does not solider, shirk, or steal? We contend that the legalistic imagery of contract enforcement is inadequate to understand the full complexity of labor control. This is what Durkheim (1997 [1893]) meant when he spoke of the "non-contractual elements of contracts." Even the most detailed of job contracts cannot specify fully all of the shared understandings, implicit expectations, and unacknowledged coercions that undergird the relationship between employer and employee in a capitalist society.

As discussed in chapter 3, labor in capitalist society increasingly takes the form of money exchanged for a person's capacity to work: that is, his or her *labor power*. But a central tenet of economic sociology is that human labor is not a commodity like any other. As Polanyi argued in his masterpiece, *The Great*

Transformation (2001 [1944]), the mechanisms through which this "fictitious commodity" is bought and sold on the market are not amenable to economic analysis alone. Rather, they require a sociological imagination attentive to the social, cultural, and political processes that enable and constrain this fiction. To this point in the book we've analyzed processes such as labor's categorization, valuation, and marketization that take place mostly outside of the workplace, in arenas such as legislatures, courts, and boardrooms. The question of labor control, however, demands that we hone our gaze even further. How, at the "point of production" itself, do employers entice people to sell their bodies and, increasingly, their souls?

Taylorism achieved great success because it offered managers a simple solution to this complex issue: hire simple people, simplify their work, and motivate them via simple incentives. But the real world and the people who inhabit it are rarely simple. Consider the fast-food franchise McDonald's, known to be the most extreme example of the application of Taylorist principles to the modern service economy. It hires mostly teenagers, pays them the minimum wage, and routinizes (i.e., "idiot-proofs") every aspect of their work. Even so, its workers are not robots. It's quite possible that one of its grillers may prepare Big Macs more slowly than do the others. The store's management could raise his wage to motivate him to work faster. But would this have the intended effect? Might it not induce him to grill even more slowly? Management could instead terminate him, but is there any guarantee that his replacement will work any faster than he did? What if the firing angers the other workers and incites them to engage in a slow-down or strike? Such questions illuminate the many dilemmas of labor control.

In this chapter we first consider the dominant approach to structuring work processes, that of finding the right mix of incentives to elicit effort. By now multiple empirical studies have shown the inadequacies of such an approach, grounded as it is in an economistic and individualistic conception of motivation. We thus consider three alternative mechanisms of control – the dispositional, the situational, and the reciprocal – that together illuminate the contentious and embedded nature of the commodity that is labor.

Beyond Sticks and Carrots

Incentives are the lynchpin of much economic and managerial thought. Behaviorist principles predict that people will repeat their actions when they are rewarded and cease them when they are punished. Of course, such assumptions are common to many traditional forms of discipline, ranging from the religious (in which the promise of salvation is supposed to motivate ethical behavior) to the familial ("spare the rod, spoil the child"). But empirical studies of actual workplaces have uncovered a multiplicity of control mechanisms, not all of them grounded in incentives (Barley and Kunda 1992). In this section we consider the supposed efficacy but also the documented failings of various incentive systems of control.

Let's start with "sticks" (i.e., negative incentives). In early, unregulated capitalism, it was common for overseers of labor to impose a range of punishments that we now find barbaric, ranging from verbal insults to involuntary confinement to physical blows. To capture the impunity with which such sanctions were delivered, sociologists have labeled such workplaces "despotic regimes" (Burawoy 1985). Today, however, the most despotic forms of discipline are universally banned, while, thanks to social protections such as unemployment insurance and basic welfare, employees generally have the option to "exit" despotic workplaces without facing dire consequences such as starvation or homelessness.

As a result, we today find truly despotic regimes only in the shadows of the formal economy, among vulnerable and unprotected populations such as undocumented immigrants or victims of human trafficking. The curtailment of such conditions is considered a matter of protecting human rights via criminal prosecution, rather than routine enforcement of labor law. Disincentives delivered via literal sticks run counter to the collective fiction of labor as a free exchange between two consenting parties. However, if current trends continue and government support for the unemployed and indigent further deteriorates, we would expect to see the reemergence of sweatshop-like conditions, even in the richest of capitalist societies.

Of course not all negative incentives are proscribed by society at large. Wage cuts, salary freezes, reductions in hours, and terminations are all deemed to be legal and legitimate under certain conditions (though these vary across societies). But how effective are these disincentives? Wages can be reduced for those who are not meeting some pre-specified performance metric, but not below the floor that is established by minimum wage laws. A worker can be dismissed, but as a means of reforming his or her job performance this is by definition not very effective. More generally, workplaces saturated with punishments tend to be characterized by low morale, which is a problem as an increasing percentage of jobs require the provision of cheerful and empathetic service (Blinder 2006).

Affecting behavior via positive incentives would seem to offer a more promising tack, but even these have been shown to be of limited effectiveness. Piece-rates, in which workers receive an hourly wage but also additional earnings for each unit they produce (usually above some baseline number), are a perfect example. They would seem to meld perfectly the principle of purchasing labor power with that of payment by results. But myriad empirical studies have shown that people do not respond to piece-rate incentives in a straight-forward way: that is, by maximizing their effort to maximize their earnings. Real workers, unlike the calculating agents supposed by much managerial theory, do not desire carrots alone.

Frederick Taylor himself was one of the first to document this phenomenon, in his treatise *The Principles of Scientific Management* (1913). In it, he tells the story of his initial attempt to eliminate soldiering at the Bethlehem Steel Works, where he'd been appointed foreman. Fresh from engineering school, he designed a piece-rate incentive system whereby workers would be rewarded for each quantity of iron that they hauled. To his surprise, however, his system produced no discernible change in work pace, a fact that, upon reflection, he attributed to entrenched bad habits among the current workforce. So Taylor went ahead and fired the entire lot, brought in a fresh batch of replacements, explained to them the logic of his piece-rate system, and trained them in the proper physical techniques for maximizing their daily output. To his puzzlement, these new workers, once they began hauling pig iron, quickly reverted back to the lackadaisical (in his opinion) pace of the previous workers.

The drama playing out at Bethlehem Steel would not have surprised the sociologist Max Weber. While Taylor thought it was illogical for people to pass up the opportunity to work harder in order to increase their pay, Weber, as we noted in chapter 2, saw this as the default human condition. In *The Protestant Ethic* he labeled this orientation to life a traditional ethos, and a good part of this classic was spent describing how early capitalists had attempted, again and again, to overcome it. Their attempts to implement piece-rate systems, for instance, were notable for the fact that they usually produced the opposite of their intended results. When managers raised the rates to stimulate additional effort, laborers would actually work less hard, content as they were to have more free time at the same amount of pay.

Both Taylor and Weber could only speculate as to why workers would not respond to incentives in the expected manner. In the decades to follow, this puzzle stimulated a good deal of research, much of it funded by big business interests (Burawoy 1979b), on workers' shopfloor culture (Dalton 1948). Some of these studies, such as the famous one of assembly workers at the Hawthorne plant of the Western Electric Company in Illinois, were conducted from a distance, by "industrial psychologists," in the form of experiments and observations. Unsurprisingly, they often reflected researchers' and funders' preexisting belief that "workers are irrational, confused, and easily manipulated by intelligent managers and that the capitalist firm is natural, nonexploitative, and potentially conflict free" (Bramel and Friend 1981: 867). Managers' quest for the holy grail – the perfect mix of incentives to counteract workers' irrationality – continued unabated.

A corrective to this one-sided view came from workplace

ethnographers: anthropologists and sociologists who actually labored for extended periods of time on the shopfloor itself, sometimes covertly, that is, with their true identities hidden from management and co-workers. As one such researcher explained: "[I] donned a diving suit and went down to see what it looked like on the bottom" (Roy 1954: 255). Such excursions revealed that incentive systems are frequently at loggerheads with the culture of workers, which seeks to preserve existing norms as to what constitutes a fair exchange of labor power for a wage (Gouldner 1964). In sum, these local shopfloor cultures constrain the individual motive to continuously maximize earnings – what Weber labeled the "ethos" of modern capitalism and Granovetter (1985) an "undersocialized" mode of action – in favor of group solidarity and stability.

Buying versus Making Dispositions

If workers cannot be bribed, perhaps they can be bought. To the extent that incentives fail to induce workers to provide the desired amount or quality of labor, an alternative is to simply purchase "better" workers in the first place. By better we do not mean more skilled or more educated. We refer instead to individuals who have either been presocialized to work in a certain way, or are pliable enough to be easily transformed in this direction (Hughes 1962).

Taylor himself proposed this technique in the wake of his prolonged struggle over piece-rates for hauling iron. He told of how, tired of haggling with current employees and their recalcitrant subculture, he instead began a search for the perfect worker. He found him in a man he called Schmidt, a burly Dutch immigrant. What made Schmidt ideal were a series of attributes that Taylor assumed were innate to his character. First, Schmidt was "close" with his money – he was by nature a sparing and thrifty man. Second, Schmidt possessed unusually high energy and stamina, which Taylor surmised by observing him "trotting . . . to work in the morning." Third, Schmidt, who spoke slowly and in broken English, possessed but a middling intellect and could thus be easily manipulated. Consider Taylor's report of his first conversation with Schmidt:

> Schmidt was called out from among the gang of pig-iron handlers and talked to somewhat in this way:
> "Schmidt, are you a high-priced man?"
> "Vell, I don't know vat you mean."
> "Oh yes, you do. What I want to know is whether you are a high-priced man or not."
> "Vell, I don't know vat you mean."
> "Oh, come now, you answer my questions. What I want to find out is whether you are a high-priced man or one of these cheap fellows here. What I want to find out is whether you want to earn $1.85 a day or whether you are satisfied with $1.15, just the same as all those cheap fellows are getting."
> "Did I vant $1.85 a day? Vas dot a high-priced man? Vell, yes, I vas a high-priced man."
> "Oh, you're aggravating me. Of course you want $1.85 a day – every one wants it! You know perfectly well that that has very little to do with your being a high-priced man. For goodness' sake answer my questions, and don't waste any more of my time."...
> "Vell, den, I vas a high-priced man."
> "Now, hold on, hold on. You know just as well as I do that a high-priced man has to do exactly as he's told from morning till night. You have seen this man here before, haven't you?"
> "No, I never saw him."
> "Well, if you are a high-priced man, you will do exactly as this man tells you to-morrow, from morning till night."...
> This seems to be rather rough talk. And indeed it would be if applied to an educated mechanic, or even an intelligent laborer. With a man of the mentally sluggish type of Schmidt it is appropriate and not unkind, since it is effective in fixing his attention on the high wages which he wants and away from what, if it were called to his attention, he probably would consider impossibly hard work. (Taylor 1913: 44–6)

Schmidt, in Taylor's account, was a perfect commodity. Strong in bone, tight in purse, and sluggish in mind, he readily followed managerial directives and did not question the basic economic logic of the piece-rate system. In addition, as an immigrant, he seemed to be isolated from the polluting influence of the work group ("these cheap fellows here").

Subsequent historical scholarship has suggested that Taylor's account of Schmidt was largely fictional (Braverman 1974). The account nonetheless had consequences, as it contributed to the emergence in the early twentieth century of an entire branch of industrial psychology dedicated to screening employees for a perfect work ethic. And even today, employers in low-wage industries prefer to hire immigrants over native-born workers out of the belief that the former are more docile and industrious (Moss and Tilly 2001). Even some sociologists have made this argument, reasoning that low-wage immigrant workers compare their jobs to prevailing salaries in their home countries, and thus are more satisfied and quiescent at work. Others point out that immigrant workers have revitalized labor unions and social movements, suggesting that their underlying dispositions are more contentious and less pliant than Taylor and others have supposed (Milkman 2006).

Among economic and organizational sociologists, the idea that one's disposition determines one's performance of a formal role has seen resurgence through Pierre Bourdieu's concept of the habitus. Bourdieu (1985) used the term – which had existed as early as the writings of Aristotle – to make sense of the accordance he observed between the objective structures of the social world and the mental structures through which actors subsequently perceive and act upon the world. It derives from an individual's initial incorporation into the primary group via language immersion, passive observation, playful imitation, and even explicit education by one's caretakers. These primordial experiences contribute to the constitution of a baseline disposition, or habitus. While all human beings possess agency and are able to learn and improvise, Bourdieu argued, these initial dispositions prove quite durable and can influence how we act in our eventual occupational and professional roles.

Bourdieu elaborated the habitus concept while studying the tribulations of peasants and workers in Algeria during the period of French colonialism. Echoing Weber, he argued that, prior to the occupation, Algerian society had been characterized by a traditional "ethos." These "technico-ritual schemes of perception and assessment" were "inculcated by material conditions of existence," namely, an agrarian economy and a social order structured around a "sense of honor" (Bourdieu 1979: 9). In the realm of production, the traditional peasant acted not as an economically rational, forward-looking actor. Rather, his "schemes of perception" were attuned to the past, and generated in him a "desire to conform to inherited models" (Bourdieu 1979: 9). His "temporal consciousness" (Bourdieu 1979: 16) was oriented not toward a future that could be imagined and changed, but toward "inherited models" demanding conformity.

So deeply entrenched was this traditional habitus that the peasant could not adjust to the stringent rhythms required by capitalist labor markets and labor processes:

> With growing adaptation to the capitalist economy and growing assimilation of the corresponding dispositions comes increasing *tensions between the traditional norms ... and the imperatives of an individualistic, calculating economy.* The sub-proletarians are subjected to contradictory pressures which give rise to ambiguous attitudes ... [and] a disorganization of conduct. (Bourdieu 1979: 48–9, italics mine)

Like the recalcitrant manual workers at Bethlehem Steel, the peasants' dispositions could not be yanked by employers out of a larger framework of traditional social meanings.

Although Bourdieu's subsequent empirical research did not return to the issues of work and labor, his theoretical writings continued to argue that one's initial habitus influences whether one accepts or challenges authority. As he states in his major contribution to economic sociology, *The Social Structures of the Economy* (2005: 130), it is the "habitus that steps in to fill the gaps in the regulation [of work]." We can see too why Bourdieu speaks of the habitus as a "wound spring" (2001: 38): a potential worker is not a raw product but an already polished commodity. He or she is "geared up," preconstituted and full of potential energy to be harnessed by those in control of the organization (and especially its selection procedures). In this perspective, the trick for management is to choose the properly wound spring to begin with. If the commodity is selected wisely and the worker's preexisting disposition matches the dictates of the work situation, techniques of control such as incentives and punishments should be rendered superfluous.

One example of this approach can be found in Hochschild's (1983) seminal study of emotional labor. Women and people from middle-class backgrounds, she argues, are overrepresented in jobs that require the conscious management of one's own emotional displays in order to invoke certain feeling-states in others. This results from the fact that these groups are socialized from an early age to constantly reflect on their own emotions and to be attentive to the emotions of others, especially their superiors. Young girls especially are taught to be considerate and caring. The family, in Hochschild's framework, becomes a veritable "training ground" (1983: 156) for the service and hospitality industries. Employers in turn do not so much investigate an applicant's objective human capital (such as grades or diplomas) as hold auditions and stage encounters in which they are able to observe applicants' "natural" personalities and dispositions. Their goal is to find those who can produce authentic emotional displays in situations of minimal supervision.

Even the training that new workers undergo may be less about learning specific skills than about tweaking their existing dispositions to match the requirements of the labor process. This was the process documented by Leidner (1993) in her ethnography of traveling insurance salesmen. Before they were sent out on their routes, the company required them to undergo an intense training program – what Leidner calls a "boot camp" – to acquire a "positive mental attitude." Teaching methods involved learning new ways to comport oneself, of managing one's body in terms of posture, appearance, and tone of voice. These are common techniques by which organizations induce members to acquire new habits of thought and attitude. And while Leidner argues that these are devices of character transformation, in truth the company had already selected employees with amendable dispositions – namely, upwardly mobile men who professed a belief in individual initiative and self-reliance.

Managerial attempts to reshape character do not cease at the training stage. For instance, many firms seek to create symbolically dense cultures that will inspire workers to subconsciously internalize the firm's goals (Podolny and Page 1998; Powell 1990). The tangible elements of these cultures, such as dinner parties and pep rallies, may look on the surface like positive incentives for good behavior. But as illustrated by the following quote, reported by Kunda (1992: 5) in his study of a high-tech company, they serve a deeper purpose: "You can't *make 'em* [i.e., employees] do *anything*. They have to want to. So you have to work through culture. The idea is to educate people without them knowing it. Have the religion and not know how they ever got it!" Just as religions cannot motivate members through fear of hell or desire for salvation alone, firms seek to manipulate organizational culture to transform employees' basic character and being.

Dispositional methods of control are not without their skeptics (Lahire 2011). Is it really possible, many ask, to remake a person's habitus? Are the testing batteries used by companies to prejudge a worker's character at all reliable? Can firms consistently predict how well potential employees will perform? One of the most famous events in labor history, known as the "Lordstown affair," suggests not. In the early 1970s, the General Motors Corporation opened a new assembly plant in a rural area of the American Midwest. The applicant pool was rigorously screened by industrial psychologists to weed out potential trouble-makers, while new hires were immersed in training programs to teach them the values of harmony and teamwork. Just a few years after the plant began operation, however, the supposedly quiescent workers became incensed at management's plan to speed up the assembly line. In response, they engaged in slow-downs, strikes, and even sabotage (Aronowitz 1973).

Others argue that dispositional theories can lead to poor sociological accounts. Like the Freudian notion of the unconscious, a habitus is not directly observable by the social scientist and can be inferred only from its effects. But this raises the danger that dispositional concepts will be mobilized to explain action in a purely *post hoc* manner ("the striking worker had a contentious habitus," "the macho worker had a masculine habitus," etc.). In response, and without reverting to an incentive-based theory of motivation, many researchers have endeavored to analyze "the mechanisms that lead frontline employees to adopt the meanings disseminated by their employers," or not (Grant et al. 2009: 327). One of these mechanisms is the constitution of the labor process as an engrossing work-game.

More Than a Game

So far we've contrasted two technologies of labor control: the provision of incentives versus the prejudgment of dispositions. Though in many ways opposed, these two approaches share an individualistic bent insofar as they seek to explain obedience through reference to the person's mind or character. The former imagines employees as calculating agents easily swayed by rewards and punishments; the latter assumes that a person's socialization determines the sort of worker he or she becomes. In contrast, an important but often overlooked body of scholarship, grounded in the symbolic interactionist tradition, directs our attention to the *situational experience of workers at work*. Its overarching thesis is that regimes of labor control are effective to the extent that they provide workers with meanings and challenges. Management, in this perspective, is like the designer of a game, and employees the players.[1]

A game is more than an assemblage of incentives. As anyone knows who has ever stayed up late into the night playing their favorite board, card, or computer game, games have the almost magic ability to make us forget about the "real world." They create an alternative reality in which we are constantly presented with puzzles to solve, quests to fulfill, and challenges to master. Other participants become teammates, competitors, and coconspirators. When it is particularly well designed, a game leads us to fully "lose ourselves" in it to the point that we scarcely are aware of the passage of time. Perhaps this was Taylor's failing. He did not realize that his piece-rate system was simply not as engrossing as were the baseball and soccer games that his workers played on the weekends.

The best-known example from this tradition is Burawoy's *Manufacturing Consent* (1979a), an ethnographic study of a Chicago engine factory. Writing from a Gramscian perspective, Burawoy posed a puzzle. Given that the exchange between capitalist and employee is exploitative (with the latter receiving less in wages than the value they produce), why did the machine operators in his factory work as hard as they did? Sure they soldiered occasionally, but most of the time they labored diligently and risked life and limb to meet or exceed the quotas. In brief, they seemed to participate enthusiastically in their own exploitation.

To explain this puzzle, Burawoy documented the "games" that workers played. Management established production quotas and employed supervisors to monitor the shopfloor, but for the most part workers were left alone at their machines. Here their actions departed from the expectations of incentive theory. Workers generally strove to exceed the baseline production quota, for doing so made them eligible for bonus pay. But they did not subsequently intensify their efforts to achieve the highest possible bonuses. If a job was "gravy" (easy), they worked more slowly than they could have; if it was a "stinker" (difficult), they were content to receive just the baseline pay. As a result, what looked to the outside observer as dull and monotonous labor was transformed into an enthralling quest to "make out." And around it formed a rich occupational subculture. Most notably, experienced operatives with a mastery of the game were looked upon with respect by their fellow workers, while newbies who worked too hard were playfully chastised.

This game, Burawoy argued, served a powerful *political function*: it legitimated exploitation. Striving to make out put the worker in an intense situation. As he battled the clock and his machine, he had no time to think about the overall commodification of his labor or the iniquitous terms of the labor exchange. He was focused on the "here and now." To state this another way, one cannot simultaneously play a game and question its rules.

But as importantly, the work game exerted a powerful *leveling effect*: it neutralized any preexisting dispositions workers may have brought into the workplace. Some operatives were better than others at making out. Some imported into the factory certain skills (e.g., physical strength) that may have helped them master the game. But in general, all workers possessed a minimal social competence that allowed them to play the game in the first place. And once it commenced, the experience of game play was so powerful that it would override any preexisting "attitudes," "beliefs," or "commitments." To prove his claim, Burawoy cited his own experience as an ethnographer. As a British sociology student, he entered the factory as a student, a foreigner, and a Marxist to boot. Of anyone, he should have been equipped with a "habitus" enabling "resistance." On the contrary, he himself soon became enthralled with playing the game, gleefully participating in his own exploitation.

A game-based theory offers a unique perspective upon the question of why regimes of labor control fail. According to incentive-based theories, control fails when rewards and punishments are not properly calibrated to employees' rationality; dispositional theories in turn assume that properly socialized employees weren't selected for the work at hand. In contrast, scholars writing in the Burawoyian tradition highlight the internal dynamics of the work situation. Managerial control becomes taken for granted, or hegemonic, to the extent that it constitutes work as an enthralling game. It follows that control will fail when the game no longer "pulls the worker in." It could be that the game has become too easy. New participants quickly master it while experienced employees are presented with no new challenges. Or it could be that the game is too difficult. It presents workers with uncertain and dangerous tasks over which they feel they have little control. In both cases, the end result is a "legitimation crisis" as bored and/or disheartened employees begin to question the larger terms of the labor exchange.

Manufacturing industries are not the only ones in which control operates via the experience of games. Pierce (1996), for example, documented the lives of professional trial lawyers. She argued that the (primarily male) lawyers worked as hard as they did not simply to maximize their earnings. Rather, they imagined themselves as combatants in a masculine status contest: "Rambo litigators" who thrived on the challenge to "'control', 'destroy', or 'rape' the witnesses" (Pierce 1996: 63). In another ethnographic study, Sallaz (2009) found that service employees can experience their work as a "game of making tips" in which they moderate how much "emotional capital" they provide clients. Because it makes their work more interesting and suspenseful, the workers he studied preferred tip income (which can be volatile) over a flat wage. Even the unemployed can experience their situation as a game of job-searching (Sharone 2007). It provides them with a sense of control over their current predicament, even if in the process it depoliticizes the inequalities present in the larger labor market.

By structuring the work process as a game, employers may be taking advantage of an innate human (and perhaps even mammalian) tendency to take pleasure in meaningful situations characterized by moderate freedom and intermittent feedback. But, as the empirical studies discussed above suggest, the specific forms of such work-games cannot be determined in advance. They will depend on the identities of individual participants, the network structure of the workgroup, the values of the larger culture, and myriad other social factors.

Is it possible to specify the conditions under which employers will attempt dispositional versus situational techniques of control? The analysis so far suggests two general hypotheses. First, dispositional approaches will be more common in the formative stage of a market economy. This was the essence of Weber's argument (2003 [1930]) concerning the birth of modern Western capitalism. Throughout history, convention and tradition had proscribed self-interested, profit-maximizing behavior. No matter what sort of material incentives or situational games were imposed, the full commodification of labor could not occur until the proper disposition was present among a critical mass of the populace. Hence the historical significance of the Protestant, or more properly

Calvinist, ethic. It glorified hard work as a way to honor God, and material wealth as a sign of salvation. As a habitus, this ethic proved transposable from the realm of religion to that of the economy, thereby bringing into being capitalism of the modern, rationalized type.

The doctrine of Calvinism, according to Weber, transformed people's dispositions so that they now thought of themselves as commodities the value of which they could and should maximize via hard labor. Once established, however, this logic of labor took on a life its own. In a free-market economy, all participants, regardless of their underlying dispositions, must play by the rules of the game. They must obtain wage labor in order to achieve a decent living, and in the workplace they will have minimal control over the conditions of their work. This was what Weber meant by his metaphor of the iron cage. The more generalizable point would be that while a change in dispositions is essential when transitioning from one social system to another, a stable social formation may be analyzed solely in terms of situational pressures upon individual behavior. In other words, the "work game" is the appropriate concept through which to view work during "settled times," while "habitus" is relevant during "unsettled times."

A second hypothesis is that while tightly regulated labor processes beget situational mechanisms of control, loosely regulated ones must permit preexisting dispositions to guide action. We may think of this as a continuum. At one end we could imagine the least free of jobs: for instance, those found in a forced labor camp. Such "total institutions" (Goffman 1961) have the power to wipe clean an occupant's past biography and unique identity. (The shaving of heads and issuance of plain uniforms frequently mark initiation into total institutions.) To understand how power operates in such a setting, we wouldn't need to know all that much about the early socialization of its workers. We could assume that such differentials are leveled, and that it is the immediate milieu of rewards, punishments, and their basic human accommodations that structure action. This argument is very much in line with that of David Swartz (1998: 113), who argues that "conduct relies less on habitus in situations that are highly codified [and] regulated."

At the other end of the continuum would be creative industries in which work is largely autonomous. We could here think of the artist painting in her studio – she literally confronts a blank canvas, and must make constant decisions (and from a wide array of options) concerning her work and style. When studying those in such positions, it makes sense to analyze the dispositions they carry with them, for these dispositions, more so than momentary or situational exigencies, are likely to shape behavior.

Of course, in the real world, most forms of work fall somewhere in between the labor camp and the artist studio, meaning that some combination of dispositional matching and situational structuring will be at play. Nor is this to be taken as an exhaustive list of control techniques. Capitalism is a dynamic system that continuously innovates new techniques for facilitating the trade of labor for money. In addition, it continues to incorporate precapitalist logics of exchange, in essence harnessing them to the yoke of wage labor. To conclude, we consider one of these: the logic of reciprocity as exemplified by the gift exchange.

On Gratitude and Effort

In his essay "Gifts," Ralph Waldo Emerson (2010 [1841]: 161) wrote, "We do not quite forgive a giver. The hand that feeds us is in some danger of being bitten." This is a disquieting image insofar as it runs counter to the commonplace notion that gifts are genuine and often spontaneous gestures of goodwill. Why would we bite the hand that offers us a present? But Emerson was pointing toward a fundamental truth that anthropologists and sociologists would subsequently elaborate in explicit theoretical terms: the principle underlying gift-giving – reciprocity – can serve as a powerful instrument of governance and even domination. In fact, many have argued that in a broad historical view, embedded reciprocity rather than calculated haggling has been the default principle structuring processes of economic exchange.

Even with capitalism now institutionalized as a taken-for-granted system, myriad everyday exchanges take the form of presents, favors, unsolicited assistance, and so on. In many contexts, gifts are bundled with regular market transactions. Consider the department store that provides shoppers a free printer with each computer they purchase, or the casino that gives complimentary dinners to gamblers. In some ways, these function as positive incentives. If debating a purchase from seller A versus seller B, the fact that seller A also includes a free add-on may sway my decision-making. But in many cases, exchange partners offer gifts *after* a transaction has been completed (Darr 2003), and even when they are unlikely to transact again in the future. The classic example is the economist who believes deeply in free-market principles, but who nevertheless offers a "gratuity" to the server at a roadside diner to which he will never return.

As the case of the tipping economist illustrates, the meanings and motivations that underlie gifting appear to run counter to those of strict market transactions. For this reason, economic sociologists and labor scholars have speculated that gifting continues to be used by employers as a method of labor control.

To see how, we can consider a broad anthropological perspective on gifting as elaborated in Mauss's work *The Gift* (1990 [1923]) and Bourdieu's *The Logic of Practice* (1990). The basic insight is that offering a gift to someone generates an expectation of a counter-gift. If you bake a pan of brownies for me on my birthday, this theory goes, I will feel a strong normative obligation to return the favor. To describe this sensation, social psychologists speak of the influence of a powerful "norm of reciprocity."[2] However, gifts represent a unique form of exchange in that the counter-gift must be both *different* and *deferred*. If a counter-gift is not different, then the entire exchange functioned simply as a loan, which may surprise the initial giver. (Imagine your reaction if I were to return to you the original, uneaten brownies on your birthday!) And if a counter-gift is not deferred, then it was simply a swap or purchase that we engaged in: you handed me some brownies and I handed you right back ten dollars.

The unique physical and temporal structure of the gift-exchange endows it with a special social efficacy. For in the time that elapses between gift and counter-gift, the recipient (R) is in debt to the giver (G). R should hold G in goodwill, look over G's flaws, be there for G, and generally behave with a sense that G is "owed one." Looked at from a political perspective, we can say that until the gift is reciprocated, G holds power over R. It is for this reason that Emerson viewed gifting as an act in need of forgiveness and Bourdieu referred to it as the paradigmatic form of "symbolic violence." It is an act of domination that is not explicitly recognized as such by either party.

In highly unequal relationships (as between a feudal lord and a serf, a village chief and a peasant, or a publicly traded firm and a low-wage worker), the asymmetry between the resources available to the giver and those available to the receiver can result in a situation of sustained domination. The superordinate party cultivates a wide network of subordinates and continuously bestows on them gifts. The latter, unable to properly reciprocate, find themselves in a state of permanent indebtedness. In such systems, social movements of the dispossessed frequently take as their rallying cry not a radical transformation of the existing order, but a simple forgiveness of their outstanding debts (Graeber 2011).

How can reciprocity function as a mechanism for motivating work? Its effects may be hard to discern to the extent that gifts are easily mistaken for basic incentives. The key difference, however, is that incentives exert their effect through a forward-looking cognition: a worker exerts effort now with the expectation of receiving a reward (or avoiding a punishment) at a future time. Reciprocity, in contrast, functions through a backward-looking morality: a worker obeys and performs out of an embodied sense of gratitude and obligation. Incentives and gift-giving, like dispositions and situational games, represent alternative logics of control.

In pre-market societies, many of the basic tasks of agriculture were understood as gift-exchanges. The seasonal nature of the work, in which crops are planted at one time period and harvested at a later one, combined with traditional religious beliefs to generate a powerful system of self-discipline:

The peasant does not, strictly speaking, labour: he takes pains. "Give [your sweat] to the earth", says the proverb. This can be taken to mean that nature, obedient to the logic of the gift exchange, grants her benefits only to those who bring her their toil in tribute. .... [T]asks of farming, such as ploughing or harvesting, impose themselves with the arbitrary rigor of traditional duties, with the same necessity as the rites which are inseparable from them. (Bourdieu 1979: 23)

To toil on the land is to engage in an extended cycle of reciprocity with nature; it is to offer it a gift that generates the counter-gift of a bountiful fall harvest, itself repaid with further labor the following spring.

Reciprocity remains alive in the modern workplace, as a mechanism by which employers control the labor of employees. Surveying the extant literature, we can discern three general forms that such gifts can take.

First, there is that of extra monetary payment. This is what Akerlof (1982: 543) meant when he spoke of "labor contracts as partial gift exchanges." A firm may decide to pay workers more than what they would be worth on the larger labor market. This extra wage is not contingent on some future level of performance (as would be a positive incentive). It is an "extra something" written into the labor contract itself, and its purpose is to make the worker feel a sense of gratitude toward her employer. This gratitude should translate, per the logic of the gift-exchange outlined above, into loyalty to the organization and a commitment to act in its interest absent any other surveillance or incentives. "My company pays me a better wage than I otherwise deserve," would go the thinking of the worker, "and so I am obligated to repay it with hard work and by being a model employee." In addition to a wage greater than market value, regular or one-off monetary payments such as holiday bonuses or stock options may instill similar sentiments.

Second, employer gifts may take the form of tangible goods and services. Examples would include the use of a company car, a card or small present on one's birthday, a fruit basket on Christmas, or complimentary coffee every morning. It is essential to recognize that these are not incentives (i.e., they are not contingent on performance), nor are they entitlements (i.e., employers are not contractually obligated to provide them). They are gestures of generosity intended to generate gratitude and effort.

But are non-monetary gifts effective? Consider an experimental study of people hired for a three-hour data entry job (Kube et al. 2011). Workers who were randomly given a thermos as a small gift before the work began exerted significantly more effort (in terms of number of characters keyed in) than those who did not receive a thermos. Notably, because the employers were clear that this was a temporary job that would not lead to permanent employment, the efficacy of the gift could not be attributed to its function as an incentive. As interesting, workers who received a thermos worked harder than did those who received cash equal to the value of the thermos. This suggests that money retains an air of payment or direct exchange, and thus remains less potent as a mechanism for motivating compliance than do gifts of a non-monetary sort.

Scholars have posited a third form that employer gifts may take: permission, usually granted implicitly, to break the official rules of the organization. Once again, we find this concept elaborated within the theoretical apparatus of Bourdieu (2005: 131), who labeled it "bureaucratic power," or the ability of an official to be flexible about the enforcement of rules. Though Bourdieu seemed to imply that bureaucratic power is less potent a mechanism for generating compliance than is selection of a properly socialized habitus, he nonetheless recognized that managers routinely deployed it as a way to motivate workers: "Holders of bureaucratic power can build up for themselves a symbolic capital that enables them ... to mobilize energies ... and thereby to achieve a kind of surplus labor and self-exploitation" (Bourdieu 2005: 132). Bourdieu's concept of bureaucratic power echoes several key ideas from the neo-Marxist scholarship of the 1970s and 1980s, notably "responsible autonomy" (Friedman 1977) and "hegemonic control" (Burawoy 1985). All of these approaches argue that when employees are granted a freedom, however minute, from direct control, they feel indebted to the firm and acts in its interests.

This third species of gift is hard to document empirically. The difference between actual and market wage rates can be calculated fairly easily, while firms are usually only too proud to promote their own largesse in the form of tangible gifts and bonuses to employees. But both employers and employees are hesitant to admit publicly that organizational rules are routinely broken, not least because some of these rules may coincide with criminal or civil law. (Consider a nursing home that allows attendants to bypass basic safety procedures or a pub that turns a blind eye to bartenders' practice of shortchanging inebriated clients.) As a result, our best evidence for the existence of bureaucratic power comes from ethnographies in which the researcher either spent long stretches of time at the point of production, or performed in-depth interviews with former employees.

An example of the former type of study would be Lee's (1998) description of the labor regime inside an electronics plant in Hong Kong. Management relied on veteran female employees to handle complex jobs. In return, these "matron workers" were allowed to violate a range of official plant rules, such as those regulating attendance and phone use, in order to attend to their family duties. An example of the latter type can be found in the work of Anteby (2008), who described an institutionalized gifting system at an aeronautics factory in France. As long as they met their production quotas, workers were permitted to use company time, tools, and materials to make their own goods. These were typically minor things, such as toys or knick-knacks, but they held sentimental value for workers, who were able to maintain an identity as independent craftsmen.

For Polanyi, the principle of reciprocity that undergirds gifting is a paradigmatic example of embedded, as opposed to rationalized, exchange. But as Bourdieu and others have argued, gifting can also be a way to create and sustain relations of domination. Like selecting incentives, choosing dispositions, and generating games, gifting is a technique of power. And like all power technologies, its efficacy is never flawless. The techniques of labor control discussed in this chapter all take as their object flesh-and-blood humans whose responses and actions can never be fully scripted or predicted in advance. Beyond individual acts of resistance, workers can and often do mobilize collectively to challenge managerial authority and the central fiction that sustains it, namely, that labor is a commodity sold by an individual alone.

7

Labor and Group-Making

The 1980s, following the previous long decade of oil shortages, tepid growth, and stagflation, witnessed a transformation in dominant paradigms of governance across many developed capitalist societies. Policies designed to buffer citizens from the ups and downs of the business cycle were abandoned as states began to experiment with market-based solutions to their many economic troubles. This neoliberal turn was especially brutal for organized labor. In the decades following the Second World War, unions grew in strength and established "labor" as a countervailing power to "big business" within regulated capitalism. Increasingly, however, unions and the collective solidarities that sustain them were viewed as anachronisms, as holdovers from an earlier and less enlightened era. Modern capitalism, held the new consensus, requires employees to imagine themselves as individual commodities competing to acquire the best jobs. Firms, in turn, should not conspire but rather bid independently to procure the services of the best and brightest workers. When both sellers and buyers of labor pursue their own interests in this manner, the overall allocation of resources in an economy is at an optimal level. Commodification, individuation, and prosperity go hand in hand.

Two confrontations from this era appeared to portend labor's imminent fall from grace. In Britain, the general term "miners' strike" will forever be tied to a specific referent: the decisive defeat of the long-powerful National Union of Mineworkers by the

Conservative government of Prime Minister Margaret Thatcher. And in the United States, labor activists still shudder at the term "PATCO," shorthand as it is for Republican President Ronald Reagan's decision to crush a strike being waged by the air traffic controllers' union. While both events were taken to sound a death knell for labor, the decades to follow did not see a complete end to collective action in these two nations. Although overall rates of unionization declined in the United States and Britain, organizers did achieve several unexpected victories. In the 1990s, for instance, unskilled (and often immigrant) janitors in both countries staged massive protests demanding better wages and working conditions. This "Justice for Janitors" campaign ("Justice for Cleaners" in Britain) challenged the neoliberal vision of atomized workers content to sell themselves at whatever price the free market dictated.

Nor was it only workers who continued to evince a taste for coordination and collective action. The neoliberal era has actually been a time of widespread corporate consolidation. Consider the highly publicized mergers between American Online and Time Warner (in telecommunications), Royal Dutch Petroleum and Shell Oil (in energy), and JP Morgan and Chase Manhattan (in banking). In fact, can there be any wonder that the 1990s were dubbed the "decade of mergers"?

Economic sociology provides several perspectives that help to explain this persistent proclivity for economic actors to form groups. For instance, some scholars emphasize that market transactions require more coordination than can be provided by market institutions alone; unions, professional associations, business groups, and the like, can actually facilitate trade (including the buying and selling of labor) by embedding transactions in cultural and moral frameworks. Others point out that it is simply quite stressful to exist in the state of constant competition required by free markets; to alleviate the associated stress and insecurity, actors agree, explicitly or implicitly, to cooperate in some way. Yet other economic sociologists argue that states continuously intervene to reinforce the fiction that employers and employees are individual entities engaged in voluntary transactions; the actions of Thatcher and Reagan, not to mention a long history of anti-trust law across capitalist economies, support this argument.

In this chapter we first survey various sociological approaches to the general phenomenon of group-making. Next, we apply these theories to the questions of why and how economic agents (both employees and employers) come to act in a collective manner. This then leads us to consider the historical arc of organized labor. Why did unions achieve widespread influence in the era of regulated capitalism, and what is labor's fate in a neoliberal era and beyond?

How to Make a Group

No concept better captures the longstanding sociological view of group-making in the workplace than the Marxist one of "class consciousness." To invoke it was to assume that the analyst could identify for each person a distinct class position within the larger capitalist mode of production; that persons similarly situated vis-à-vis ownership of the means of production would share a mutual interest; and that if individuals did not band together to act on their shared interests, they suffered from an inauthentic, or false, class consciousness. The imagery suggested by a term such as false consciousness is that of a shroud placed before workers' eyes that prevents them from seeing reality as it is and from thus joining together with the similarly situated.

The class consciousness concept was often productive for scholarship and theorizing. It opened debate as to the conditions under which workers would opt to engage in collective action, and it raised the question of who specifically is best positioned to serve as an agent of "consciousness-raising" for a given class fraction. Too often, however, class consciousness was treated as an individual-level property and operationalized via survey questionnaires as a "belief" or, even worse, an "attitude." More recent work in economic, political, and cultural sociology has redirected focus from class as cognitive "consciousness" to class-making as a contingent process embedded in institutional contexts, representational dilemmas, and lived experience.

Above and beyond the mind of any one individual there lies a political-institutional domain that establishes the very possibility of collective action. States are important actors in this domain, insofar as they monopolize the authority to decide what forms of association are to be deemed legitimate. States also establish the channels by which groups may coalesce, accumulate resources, voice their grievances, interact with one another, and disband. Over time, these forms of political intervention become institutionalized as national or regional specific employment systems. These systems are not immutable, but they are durable. Once in place they establish a framework within which subsequent mobilization and bargaining occur, a phenomenon known as path-dependency (Thelen 2004).

Empirical work has documented variation across capitalist societies in terms of predominant patterns of collective action and their associated employment systems. The United States, for instance, has historically been a nation in which private firms are acknowledged to be the key actors in the economy; managers acquire a strong collective ethos owing to their common training in business schools; and organized associations of employees are either coopted by firms ("company unions") or treated as adversaries ("union-busting").

The US system contrasts with that found in much of Europe. In Germany, for instance, trade unions are more often treated as partners in industrial governance, while collective bargaining between unions and employers is taken for granted. Furthermore, managerial identities are grounded in a vocational ethic and are thus not as hostile to workers. As Fligstein (2001a: 106) explains, the "distinction between management and workers is not as strong in such systems, since the management function is less professionalized and since lower management often is recruited from the rank of workers." According to the logic of political institutionalism, ongoing national differences such as those that exist between the United States and Germany can be traced back to struggles and coalitions among "the players involved in the formation of employment systems" (Fligstein 2001a: 120).

A second critique of the class consciousness model is that

it inadequately theorizes the cultural and symbolic nature of group-making. Collectivities are never simply aggregates of their individual members. To be recognized as a group, members must do several things. They must, for example, subsume their myriad individual attributes to a single group identity (as expressed through the display of symbols such as a coat of arms, a logo, or a mascot). And they must designate certain individuals to represent them and speak in their interests. A union, for instance, cannot in its entirety testify before Parliament or sit at a bargaining table. Instead, authority to represent and speak for the group must be delegated to some person. Though he is not normally associated with the study of labor, the sociologist Bruno Latour (1988: 72) offers an interesting illustration of how this process works:

> The spokesperson is someone who speaks for others who, or which, do not speak. For instance a shop steward is a spokesman. If the workers were gathered together and they all spoke at the same time there would be a jarring cacophony. . . . This is why they designate (or are given) a delegate who speaks on their behalf, and in their name. The delegate – let us call him Bill – does not speak in *his* name and when confronted with the manager does not speak "as Bill" but as the "workers' voice". . . . The voice of the floor, articulated by Bill, wants a "3 per cent pay rise – and they are deadly serious about it, sir, they are ready to strike for it," he tells the manger. The manager has his doubts: "Is this really what they want? Are they really so adamant?" "If you don't believe me," replies Bill, "I'll show you["] . . . What does the manager see? He does not see what Bill said. Through the office window he simply sees an assembled crowd gathered in the aisles. Maybe it is because of Bill's interpretation that he reads anger and determination on their faces.

This hypothetical situation raises several important questions germane to the study of group-making in and around the workplace – what Bourdieu called the "mystery of ministry" (Wacquant 2005). How does a group select a particular agent to be its spokesperson? How do spokespersons mobilize their constituencies in key moments such as in direct negotiation with an employer (an element of what Fligstein [2001b] refers to as "social skill" within a field)? How can the group make sure that the spokesperson authentically represents it and does not abuse the power they have entrusted him or her with? (In Gramsci's [1971] terms, this is the dilemma of ensuring that the leader remains organically linked to the class.)

Such questions take us well beyond a model of *individual* class consciousness. But this should not be taken to suggest that an economic sociology of labor would gloss over the reasons why people *do* decide to form groups. At some point, a worker has to cast a vote for or against unionization, opt to go on strike or not. And it is true that for any individual, joining an association has economic cost and benefits. But these are not easily calculated and compared. For instance, unionized workplaces on average offer higher wages than do their non-union counterparts; but it's also true that union members have to pay regular dues out of their paychecks. The right to unionize is protected by the UN Charter on Human Rights; but employers often fire with impunity those workers who support a union. The calculations that workers make in regard to matters like unionization, research suggests, are inadequately captured by a model of self-interested, forward-looking individuals pursuing economic gain. In the spirit of E. P. Thompson's classic work on the "*making* of the English working class" (1966: emphasis mine), we argue that an individual's decision to engage in collective action must be studied via a contextual understanding of his or her lived experience.

The idea that one's biography shapes one's orientation toward unionization is a central thesis of Lopez's (2004) ethnography of underpaid nursing aides in a depressed industrial region of the United States' "rust belt." Though they seemed to have nothing to lose and everything to gain by forming a union, these workers nonetheless exhibited a visceral aversion to the very idea of unionization. Mainly women and ethnic minorities, they had long since formed an image of unions as corrupt and of union leaders as "bosses" who would extort them into striking and paying exorbitant dues. It was only by slowly building up trust and demonstrating in concrete, practical ways what it is that unions do that organizers were able to reconfigure workers' deep understandings of collective action.

The lived experience of collective action depends as well on the composition of one's personal networks. As Fantasia (1988) argues, the fateful decision to cast one's lot in with one's peers emanates not simply from coalitions of individuals who share the same material interests, but from vibrant "cultures of solidarity." The traditional image of such a culture was the closely knit working-class neighborhood in which the young generation took pride in following in the footsteps of its forebears by learning a craft and joining the union. More recently, scholars have posited that cultures of solidarity may be more dispersed. They may operate through common membership in voluntary associations such as book clubs, civic organizations such as churches, or even social media such as Facebook. In each case, people internalize meanings and make normative judgments about unions in accord with the sentiments of those with whom they routinely interact.

Unions in turn draw strength from members' networks. If members are well integrated into their communities, they can easily communicate among themselves and can also pass along information to outsiders about the mission of their union and its activities. Conversely, in situations in which existing union members have few network ties and are members of few other organizations, it becomes more difficult to recruit new members and garner sympathy for the union's activities (Cornwell and Harrison 2004). Isolation mutes the possibility of struggle, a fact pointed out by the feminist scholar Simone de Beauvoir (2011 [1949]) in regard to the dilemma of women in the early twentieth century. Unlike male workers, who were being herded into factories and forced to intermingle, women were isolated in the household and so had fewer opportunities to communicate among themselves, share their experiences, and learn the merits of collective action.

No discussion of how collective action is embedded within lived experience would be complete without a consideration of the power of larger narratives of justice, equity, and fairness. Mobilization, many argue, follows less from explicit calculation of costs and benefits, and more from the stories that people tell themselves about their worlds. These stories provide answers to questions such as: What is the source of my problems? Who is at fault? How can they be remedied? As noted by C. Wright Mills (2000 [1959]), humans have a tendency to tell themselves personal stories grounded in their local milieu; it is a learned skill to be able to situate one's personal troubles within historical and structural contexts. Skillful organizers in turn craft narrative "frames" that give potential members a vocabulary through which to diagnose their predicaments and imagine potential remedies (Benford and Snow 2000). The power of such stories is amplified when told in actual group settings, where they energize participants and inspire solidarity (Polletta 2006).

United, Employers Stand

Thus far the discussion has made collective action by workers its implicit focus. But we should not neglect to consider the possibility of association among employers, and its consequence for the structuring of work.

Classical social theory offers two contrasting visions of employer association, which we can call the anarchic and the conspiratorial. The former is associated with Marx, who viewed constant competition among producers as a defining feature of capitalism. Isolated from and jealous of his brethren, the capitalist fights a never-ending though ultimately futile battle to stay ahead of the game:

> [T]he *privileged position* of [a] capitalist is not of long duration; other competing capitalists introduce the same machines, the same division of labor, introduce them on the same scale or on a larger scale, and this introduction [becomes] general. . . . That is the law which again and again throws bourgeois production out of its old course and which compels capital to intensify the productive forces of labour . . . the law which gives capital no rest and continually whispers in its ear: "Go on! Go on!" (Marx 1978b [1849]: 213)

In turn, attempts by capitalists to form trusts or monopolies expose the inherent flaws of the system and only speed up the transition to socialism and, eventually, communism.

The counter-argument is that even capitalists eventually tire of having no rest, and will opt to conspire among themselves to restrict competition in some way. This was the view of Adam Smith (1904 [1776], sec. I.10.82), who argued that "[p]eople of the same trade seldom meet together, even for merriment and diversion, but the conversation ends in a conspiracy against the public." And because "[i]t is impossible indeed to prevent such meetings," the government can at best attempt to regulate the most extreme and pernicious restraints on competition.

Findings from economic sociology have tended to support the latter argument, though not in its extreme conspiratorial form. We can specify three broad classes of mechanisms by which coordination is achieved in actual producer markets: consolidation, networks, and fields. Consolidation is the most visible manifestation of coordination, taking the form of mergers, buyouts, cartels, and bankruptcies that leave one or a handful of firms in control of the market. There very well may be an inherent tendency toward monopolies and oligopolies in producer markets, such that the main constraint on their constitution must come from some exogenous entity. More often than not, this is the state.

Historically, we find that states can take a range of stances toward producer consolidation. In the United States and other market-oriented societies, judicial bodies and regulatory agencies have banned them as tyrannical threats to the common good; while in capitalist societies featuring a strong bureaucracy and powerful executive, such as France, they may be encouraged, chartered, and then brought under the auspices of the central state (Dobbin 1997; Dobbin and Dowd 2000). And in industrializing economies, government officials may seek to foster growth by favoring local producers and protecting them from the external market (Hirschman 1968). Alternatively, they can privilege investment from foreign firms by providing them with low-tax and union-free "export process zones" (McKay 2006) or offering them "substantive legitimacy" within the existing political order (Bandelj 2009a). In either case, protectionism can lead to a situation where industry grows too powerful and captures the state for its own purposes (Evans 1995).

Producer networks refer to any tangible relationships that exist among economic agents and which mitigate the pressures of direct, constant competition. Some of these are quite obvious, such as lobbies, business groups, chambers of commerce, or industry-specific associations (Keister 2000). Others are less visible and more difficult to prove empirically, requiring specially created data sets (and often scientific methods of network mapping). Examples include common participation by elites in social organizations such as country clubs, charities, or alumni groups; overlapping membership on corporate boards (Mizruchi 1992); and repeated patterns of trade that generate familiarity and trust (Macaulay 1963; Uzzi 1997).

Field-based forms of coordination are perhaps the least apparent to the naked eye. They exist as implicit understandings among market actors as to the rules of the game and the forms of behavior that are acceptable. These "conceptions of control" (Fligstein 2001a) turn potentially anarchic markets into stable social structures. Importantly, they establish a hierarchy in which established actors dominate the field through their control of various forms of capital (money, but also prestige, knowledge, and political influence). In turn, smaller and less established firms survive (and often thrive) by occupying positions at the margins of the field. They do not compete directly with dominant firms, but rather satisfy niche tastes or specialize in non-standard methods of production.

Disruptions to an established market field can come from various sources. Peripheral firms may grow dissatisfied with their dominated status and seek to usurp incumbents, while opportunities to do so may arise from events exogenous to the field itself. This would be an apt description of the automobile market in the United States during the twentieth century. It had been long dominated by a trio of firms known as the "Big Three" (Ford, General Motors, and Chrysler) producing for the mass market, with various small producers, many of them based in Europe and Asia, satisfying niche tastes such as for luxury or fuel-efficient cars. The oil embargo of the 1970s, however, caused gasoline prices to skyrocket. Several of the former niche producers, especially Honda and Toyota, grasped the opportunity. They marketed directly to mainstream consumers and contrasted their products to those of the Big Three. Today, they are among the dominant actors in the field.

Fields may also be altered via direct intervention by the state. Law-makers, courts, and other political actors may prevent firms from coordinating their behavior through the enforcement of anti-trust laws. Changes in accounting rules, bankruptcy law, and tax policies may encourage or discourse mergers and acquisitions (Halliday and Carruthers 2007). And systems of property rights can foster or restrict competition (Stark 1996).

Let's turn now to the issue of how coordination in a given market relates to firms' strategies for managing labor. Sociological thought has generally been of two minds on this issue. Some maintain that unity among employers equates to worsened conditions for workers. In this argument, firms coordinate among themselves to maintain wage ceilings; they agree not to engage in bidding wars for skilled employees; they share information to blacklist troublesome workers or union agitators; and they can lobby effectively to pass legislation favorable to industry vis-à-vis workers.

Conversely, many have argued that employees actually fare better under conditions of employer solidarity. In this view, it is the intense pressure of competition that drives firms to exploit workers. When margins are slim, firms are more likely to treat labor costs as a variable and to value short-term profits over long-term continuity. To paraphrase Marx, anarchy in the market equates to despotism in the factory. This line of argumentation is often used to understand the system of labor relations under monopoly capitalism, or Fordism. As US auto firms embraced Taylorist principles of work routinization early in the twentieth century, disgruntled workers engaged in actions including a series of famous sit-down strikes at a GM plant in Flint, Michigan in 1936 and 1937. With their monopoly market power, firms opted to recognize the union. The subsequence collective bargaining agreements regulated the conditions under which workers could legitimately strike, but workers in turn received generous wages and regular raises. Industrial peace and prosperity lasted until the reintroduction of competition via global events of the 1970s. Since then, firms have forced unions to agree to multiple concessions, such as lower wages and increased outsourcing (Sallaz 2004).

In sum, there is no firm agreement on how consensus (versus competition) among firms affects labor. Most likely the relationship is contingent upon various other factors, such as the role of the state and the larger global context. Any historical account of the changing balance of power between employees and employers, labor and capital, must take these factors into consideration.

The Rise of Labor

To the extent that human labor is transformed into a basic commodity, Polanyi (2001 [1944]) argued, workers are degraded and dehumanized. One way in which workers can counter the deleterious effects of such commodification is by organizing and acting *en bloc*. What this does is regulate the various facets of the employment relationship – from hiring criteria to wage determination to termination procedures – in line with principles other than those of the free market. More generally, it transforms employment from a one-to-one exchange to a collective institution. Earlier, we discussed some general principles governing the process of group-making. In this section, we examine broad historical trends of unionization from an economic-sociological viewpoint.

Is it possible to summarize in one narrative arc the history of unions (and other employee associations) in capitalist societies? At the risk of oversimplifying a complex issue, we can say that the rise of an industrial-market economic order stimulated a vibrant union movement across nation-states, while the emergence of a neoliberal global order since the 1980s has seen the size and influence of unions wane.

The story of the rise of the labor movement is often associated with almost mythical imagery of alienated and abused workers waking up and fighting back against abusive bosses. And there is more than a grain of truth to this narrative. The first factories featured foremen who relied upon primitive forms of discipline to "drive" and "sweat" workers. Governments provided workers with few protections; in fact, during labor disputes, state resources were often mobilized to violently suppress workers. In these circumstances, those who stood up and spoke out for unionization exhibited great courage and put much at risk – including their own lives. In adopting a sociological perspective, we seek to understand some of the more basic processes that account for why so many employees succeeded against long odds in having their unions recognized. We evoke two concepts from the literature on social movement organizations: resource mobilization and political opportunities.

Unions and other employee associations attempt to advance the interests of their members. Often, if not always, their claims conflict with the interests of employers, owners, and managers. It would be an understatement to say that workers are "outgunned" in these struggles from a financial perspective. Even if they were to pool all of their assets, it is unlikely that they could match the resources of a publicly traded corporation or even a large family firm (Fligstein and Fernandez 1988). To understand how and why workers can and do prevail despite this asymmetry of financial resources, sociologists have proposed three sources of power that workers *do* possess (Wright 2000).

First is a form of leverage known as workplace power. It derives from a given group of workers' location in a given production process, and refers to the negative consequences that would follow should they cease working or otherwise disrupt the normal flow of production. If you've ever wondered, "What would happen if I didn't show up to work today?" you've pondered your own workplace power.

But not all workers possess this power to the same degree. It is in essence a variable, a fact with important implications for workers' ability to form unions and to bargain with employers (Dixon et al. 2004). Prior to the advent of mass production, factory owners were reliant on craftsmen and artisans who alone knew the intricacies of how things were made. This knowledge constituted a resource that could be used to extract concessions from employers. But as routinization, specialization, and Taylorism slowly eroded the bases of craft knowledge, the balance of power shifted.

Work was deskilled and each worker performed but a minor task in a much larger production process. The image of a lone worker tightening lug nuts on a vast assembly line illustrates this enfeebling: Would it really matter if he walked off the job? Couldn't the company find someone to replace him in a heartbeat?

It was one of the paradoxes of Fordism that at the same that it deskilled work, it strengthened the workplace power of workers. It did so by tightly "coupling" the various stages of the production process. Just as Perrow (1999 [1984]) argued that complex organizational systems are prone to accidents such as nuclear meltdowns and oil spills because a failure in one area quickly spreads to others, the Fordist assembly system integrated multiple subassembly systems into a single whole and so was vulnerable to small but strategically sited industrial actions. This is why a small band of workers whose job it was to make sparkplugs could strike and, in so doing, shut down the entire production process throughout a major auto company and potentially even cripple the entire economy (Helper 1991).

Conceptualizing workplace power as a variable also helps to explain what would otherwise appear a curious pattern: an increased prevalence of collective employee action during times of war. A team led by the sociologist Beverly Silver (2003) scoured hundreds of newspapers for all years since 1870, in order to create a database of all reported strikes, sit-ins, demonstrations, and other examples of "labor unrest" in industrial economies. While one might assume that patriotism would trump economic concerns during wartime as citizens suppress their own interests in service of a larger mission, the data reveal the opposite: unrest peaked dramatically around the two world wars (i.e., from 1915 to 1920 and from 1940 to 1948), before leveling off at a fairly high level up until the 1980s.

From this data one could surmise that workers were strategically taking advantage of a political opportunity. During times of war, states prioritize a steady flow of industrial output, especially as non-defense sectors of the economy are converted for military production. This increases the leverage of workers, who are temporarily in a position to extract greater concessions from firms. A

147

good deal of historical evidence suggests that states are more likely to intervene in labor disputes during wartime in order to broker industrial peace, and that, given the larger imbalance of power between workers and firms, such intervention is usually beneficial for workers.

The case of state intervention illustrates a second source of strength for workers, their associational power. This refers to workers' ability to organize themselves (e.g., into unions), but also to their capacity to liaise with other groups such as political parties, community groups, and social movements. The benefits of such association are clear. For instance, by forming multiple allies, workers can push to oppose legislation that is against their interests. This was the case during a 2011 dispute in the US state of Wisconsin, where Republican governor Scott Walker sought to reform the law to restrict the collective bargaining rights of state employees. In response there mobilized a broad coalition of groups opposed to the neoliberal principles underlying the proposed policy change. In coordination with the union representing state employees, they occupied the state courthouse and collected thousands of signatures for a petition to recall the governor. Although Walker ultimately survived the recall motion, the events in Wisconsin demonstrated that workers could generate wide support for their struggles to maintain their rights and benefits at work.

Organized labor can also participate in mobilizations for or against policy changes that may not affect workers directly. In the aftermath of the global financial crisis originating in 2008, governments across Europe proposed austerity measures to cut financing for various public services. Unions and trade groups were among many collective actors to protest these cuts, even putting to use their workplace power by striking and disrupting transportation networks. Cuts to public services of course do affect the working class indirectly. But by eliminating support for the unemployed, the state effectively pushes a larger swath of people to commodify themselves in the labor market. (To state this another way, an increase in public services serves to decommodify labor, by making people less reliant on wage work to sustain themselves.) But what is significant is the way in which organized groups of workers built their associational power by aligning themselves with a broader movement for social justice (Clawson 2003). And of course not all such associations of labor and community groups are so dramatic. More common though less visible are the many local coalitions among unions, charities, churches, environmental groups, and other institutional actors.

We have come a long way from the image of atomized workers selling their labor to an individual employer. But the concept of associational power has also been used to explain divergent trajectories of working-class influence across nation-states. Often the United States is contrasted with Western and Northern Europe. The latter are home to established labor parties which field candidates for office and are generally integrated into the political machinery (Berggren 1994). The labor movement in the United States, in contrast, has historically stayed out of the political arena, opting instead to confine its influence to the workplace. "American exceptionalism" has been attributed to a variety of causes. Some emphasize the moderate dispositions of early union leaders and their ability to suppress more radical elements within the labor movement (Lichtenstein 1997). Others point to the high degree of political decentralization that characterized the United States during its initial phase of proletarianization. Unlike their European counterparts, who had to consolidate as political parties to challenge absolutist rulers and powerful central states, American workers restricted their sphere of influence to local politics and the shopfloor itself (Katznelson and Zolberg 1986).

Associational power also helps to explain the unique forms that worker movements have taken in the global South. Western powers colonized these societies for a variety of reasons, from land acquisition to resource extraction to the securing of trade routes. In some cases the societies were ruled from afar (so-called administrative colonies) and in some cases via the establishment of permanent outposts (settler colonies). In nearly every case, however, indigenous peoples were both dehumanized by racial ideologies of white supremacy (Fredrickson 1982) and incorporated into the labor force as workers (though to varying degrees and in various forms depending upon the overall nature of the colony).

Given these dual bases of oppression – as a denigrated social caste and an exploited working class – we can see how and why movements to organize labor unions in the colonies could hardly have confined their focus to workplace struggles alone. In fact, worker movements and nationalist independence movements often developed hand in hand. As Seidman (1994: 11) observed, "[U]nder conditions of . . . authoritarian industrialization, organizations rooted in workplace relations could hardly resist pressures to take up issues outside the factory." We thus find that independence movements succeeded when they were able to harness the workplace power of union members, while unions built up their associational power and were integrated into the postcolonial orders.

An excellent example is the wave of industrial actions that shook Durban, South Africa in 1972–3. Ninety thousand black workers went on strike to protest the infamous and well-institutionalized system of discrimination known as the "color bar." This set off a chain of events. Employers capitulated in the face of such a widespread exercise of workplace power by loosening restrictions on black trade unions. The newly legitimated unions then built up their associational power by collaborating with the political arm of the black independence movement, the African National Congress, or ANC. Following the ANC's victory in South Africa's first democratic elections in 1994, apartheid came to an end and the Congress of South African Trade Unions, or COSATU, was brought into the political system as part of a formal governing alliance.

Workplace power and associational power are distinct from a third form of leverage: marketplace power. This refers to the ability of the incumbent members of a given occupation to restrict the number of new entrants into the trade. The benefits of doing so are clear: fewer suppliers of labor (i.e., employees) hinder the relative bargaining power of buyers (employers). The notion of marketplace power explains also why employers have an interest in deskilling labor: by making jobs simpler and simpler, the pool of potential employees increases and the bargaining power of existing employees decreases. Yet the story of how, historically, workers have managed to close off entry to their trades is one that invariably leads to consideration of political factors. Two general paths, exhibiting different trajectories, can be identified.

The first is the pathway pursued by semi-skilled, low-skilled, and unskilled workers, which is to impose some variation of a "closed shop." This means that an employer can hire an employee only if he or she has first joined the relevant trade union. Practically, it entails a usurpation of the employer's prerogative to draw labor from the larger market, by establishing the union as the key intermediary between employers and employees. Less extreme versions of this system are the "union shop," in which employers can hire whom they please but all new workers have to join the union shortly thereafter, and the "hiring hall," in which employers retain formal control of the hiring process but rely on union referrals to fill all new openings. In certain situations, other employee groupings besides those of a labor union can serve this function, as when a particular trade is monopolized by a particular ethnic group which then controls entry into the trade by, for instance, guarding access to hiring channels or selectively distributing information about new job openings.

The greater the extent to which a workplace relies on low-skilled labor, the more puzzling it appears as to why employers would agree to a closed-shop provision to begin with. One straight-forward answer is that states play a major role in regulating closed-shop scenarios. If they are sanctioned and protected by law, they may prove durable and may even become institutionalized as taken for granted; but if they are not, they should prove to be highly unstable and ephemeral. The case of the United States would certainly fit the latter scenario. In 1935, President Franklin D. Roosevelt signed a piece of legislation known as the Wagner Act, which allowed unionized workers to form closed-shop arrangements and, as importantly, to engage in solidarity strikes with other unions. In 1947, however, Congress passed (over a presidential veto) a new federal law known as the Taft–Hartley Act, which deemed illegal the closed-shop arrangement, disallowed solidarity striking, and granted individual states the ability to further protect an individual's "right to work."

A second path to marketplace power is the one pursued by professional workers who claim some special expertise, insofar as they are able to police the internal and external boundaries of their profession. By policing internal boundaries, we refer to two things: control over the criteria for entering the profession, such as when medical doctors establish entrance exams that one must pass in order to be certified as competent in the field; and the capacity to foster a corporatist identity among members, for instance by forming an association or having all members take an oath of membership. By policing external boundaries, we also refer to two separate ideas: the profession's ability to counter threats to its own legitimacy, as the medical profession has vis-à-vis challenges from homeopathic medicine (Scott et al. 2000); and the profession's capacity to grow by generating new knowledge and expanding the range of problems to which its expertise applies (Brint 1996).

As Abbott (1988) and others have argued, obtaining professional autonomy (and the benefits of occupational closure that this entails) depends on receiving legitimacy from the state. The transition from absolutism, in which sovereigns ruled in order to maximize their own wealth and honor, to that of governmentality (Foucault 1980), in which leaders derive authority by pledging to protect and nurture the population, witnessed the emergence of a "social activist state" (Garth and Sterling 1998). One key pillar of this new conception of governance was the state's role in protecting consumers from unscrupulous proprietors, unsafe goods and services, and other perils of the free market (Seabrooke 2006). In this sense the modern state and the knowledge-based professions emerged hand in hand. States increasingly sought to regulate supply by certifying standards for entry into producer-fields, while producers themselves increasingly sought to self-organize by monopolizing knowledge and expanding their domains.

The Fall of Labor

The current world of work is one in which collective action on the part of employees is waning. Whether you are blue-collar,

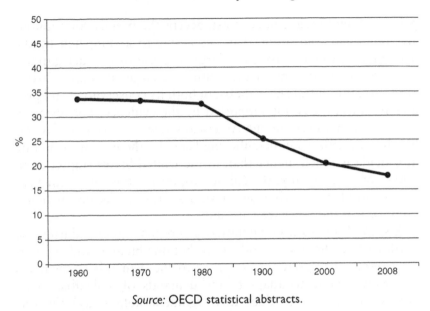

Source: OECD statistical abstracts.

Figure 7.1 Unionization rate in OECD countries, 1960–2008

pink-collar, or white-collar, the chances are growing increasingly slim that you will be part of a formal organization, such as a labor union, that represents and advocates for your interests. Consider changes in the overall rate of unionization since 1960 among workers in the 34 countries that comprise the Organization for Economic Co-operation and Development (OECD), an international forum for the world's major capitalist economies (see figure 7.1).

Beginning around 1980, the unionization rate began to drop. Today it is around 17 percent, half of what it was three decades ago, when one-third of all workers were members of labor unions. Many observers have attempted to explain this decline. Some conservative thinkers argue that it reflects the fact that unions are an archaic and unpopular institution in the world today. As people become more modern, entrepreneurial, and individualistic, they do not want to associate with labor unions. The image of "union men" marching on a picket line no longer appeals to the popular palate. Many liberals, in contrast, accept the premise that unions are unpopular, but argue that this is due to a campaign by the mass media (itself controlled by large corporations) to delegitimize workers' organizations in the culture at large (Richards 2010). However, this culture-war thesis, in both its conservative and progressive variants, is not supported by the evidence. For instance, polls show that even though Americans view unions more favorably than do citizens in neighboring Canada, the unionization rate in Canada is much higher than in the United States (Lipset et al. 2004). More generally, the culture argument runs into a chicken-or-egg problem: do changes in values cause a decline in union rates, or is it the other way around?

A second line of argumentation posits that unions, during the heyday of Fordist mass production, became bloated and corrupt. As a result, they grew unresponsive to the demands of members and were unable to adapt to the demands of a flexible, post-Fordist economy. But does this argument hold sway? On one hand, unions are certainly not immune from what Michels (2012 [1911]) labeled the "iron law of oligarchy," whereby increasing size and bureaucratization tend to lessen political responsiveness to the membership. But, on the other hand, the archetypical bureaucratic actor of the twentieth century – the publicly traded firm – was no stranger to corruption and inefficiency (Roy 1999), yet it has survived well into the twenty-first (DiMaggio 2003). Furthermore, many labor unions have redesigned themselves to become less bureaucratic and more responsive (Voss and Sherman 2000), with no noticeable effect upon the larger statistical trend of union decline.

To gain some traction on the issue, we can break down the decline in union density across multiple OECD countries (see figure 7.2). While all witnessed sizable drops, the countries sort into two groups. On one side, losses were particularly stark in the United States (19 percent), Germany (16 percent), Japan (14 percent), France (12 percent), and the United Kingdom (12 percent). In contrast, losses were less severe in Norway (7 percent), Sweden (4 percent), and Canada (2 percent).

In thinking about why the latter countries have bucked the

Labor and Group-Making

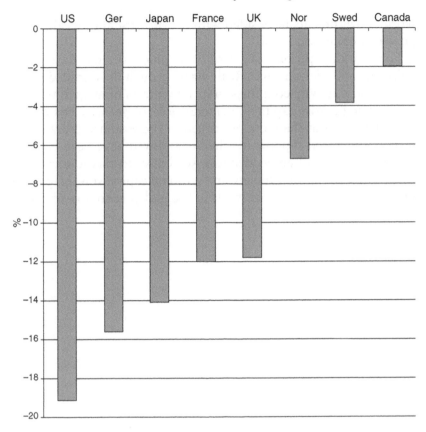

Source: OECD statistical abstracts.

Figure 7.2 Union decline across select OECD countries, 1960–2008

larger trend, we should note that these are large net exporters of natural resources such as oil and timber. As compared to manufacturing and services, these sectors are more insulated from the pressures of globalization. But political factors are also at play (Kwon and Pontusson 2010). In interpreting cross-national patterns of union decline, the sociologist Bruce Western (1999) steers away from blaming union bureaucracy or shifting values. He instead points to how well incorporated unions are into the political system in Northern Europe. In much of the rest of the capitalist world, governments have sided with private capital to weaken the power of organized labor.

For working people, the results of union decline have been palpable and deleterious. Real wage growth has stalled even though productivity continues to increase; rates of inequality have skyrocketed across capitalist democracies; job security has disappeared for all but the most privileged of professions; and various forms of material support for the unemployed have been eroded. Can the concept of embeddedness, so central to classic sociological accounts of market society and national capitalisms, help us to understand the position of work in the global economy of today and tomorrow?

8

Conclusion:
What Good is Embeddedness?

At the heart of capitalism's inhumanity – and no sensible person will deny that the market is an amoral and often cruelly capricious master – is the fact that it treats labor as a commodity. (Krugman 1999: 15)

We live at a time in which myriad forces conspire to convince us that our labor is a commodity like any other. The various components of our education – the books we read, the lectures we attend, the essays we write – are to be thought of as but means to maximize our human capital. Upon graduation we should seek not service in a meaningful calling, but employment in a field that maximizes the return on our investment. The job search itself becomes a heroic quest undertaken by each of us individually, and the hiring process a negotiation, *mano-a-mano*, between ourselves and a potential employer. The economist Paul Krugman, by labeling this process a cruel and capricious one, swims against the dominant ideological current. Even in the midst of crisis, few dispute the idea that the logic of the market, like the invisible hand postulated by Adam Smith, will channel each of us toward the greatest wealth and happiness.

This book has sought to challenge the premise that human labor is, in its essence, a commodity that exists to be exchanged on the open market. What Simmel, in the book's opening epigraph, referred to as the *"real process* which one understands as labor" rests upon non-economic foundations. We have discussed a number that we believe to be central: an initial legitimation of capitalist labor markets (chapter 2); the establishment of "work" as a valid cultural category (chapter 3); metrics and codes for commensurating human labor with other substances (chapter 4); the bounded rationality of employer–employee matching processes (chapter 5); the innovation of non-economic means for coaxing effort from workers (chapter 6); and the persistence of collective action at work (chapter 7).

The concept of embeddedness, more so than any other, has grounded the lexicon of the emergent field of economic sociology. Some (e.g., Barber 1995; Krippner 2001) have criticized economic sociologists on precisely these grounds: they have used the term so often and to signify so many different things that it has lost its conceptual precision. Social networks, cognitive fallacies, institutional logics, global norms, cultural understandings – all of these and more have been said to embed the economy in one way or another. As definitions proliferate, embeddedness becomes a platitude or, worse, a slogan. Its usage then obscures more than it reveals about real economic processes, such as those constitutive of labor under capitalism.

We agree with the thrust of this critique, and have herein sought to restrict our use of the embeddedness concept accordingly. Our point of departure was Polanyi's insight that basic economic functions of production and exchange cannot but be embedded in larger institutions. One such institution is a free market grounded in self-interested profit-seeking along with a price mechanism that establishes equivalences and regulates exchange. Historically, however, it was unthinkable to organize an entire society on the basis of free-market institutions. Instead, people relied on institutions such as reciprocity, in which goodwill and mutual obligation unite exchange partners, and redistribution, in which a central authority coordinates production and distribution. It's not that systems of reciprocity and redistribution were idyllic Edens free of power, abuse, and exploitation. It's rather the case that the principles underlying these systems were more in line with the values and norms of human communities than were those undergirding a market system.

Polanyi meant markets, reciprocity, and redistribution as ideal types. That is, they are unlikely to be found in a pure state, with existing societies exhibiting some mixture of the three (Block 2003). Failure to recognize this may be at the root of the confusion that has plagued economic sociologists' use of the embeddness concept. On one hand, it is not that market institutions were absent from the non-capitalist world. Historical, anthropological, and sociological research, for instance, has revealed the use of cash-based exchange systems in ancient temples, blood feuds, dowry settlements, and Soviet factories. But on the whole, free-market institutions were stigmatized and their use was restricted in these societies.

On the other hand, it does not invalidate Polanyi's larger argument to point out that non-market institutions persist in market societies. Nor should we be surprised to discover that many market transactions seem to be intertwined with cultural meanings, social relationships, and political maneuvering. Indeed, such observations have suffused this book. Labor can function as a commodity only if states establish employment as a valid cultural category; markets for labor rely on networks and heuristics; employers exert control by giving gifts to employees; and so on. In fact, all of these characteristics of labor are consonant with Polanyi's initial use of the embeddedness concept, and documenting them empirically will continue to constitute an essential task of a critical economic sociology of labor.

But perhaps the time has come to move beyond embeddedness, to instead put at the center of our agenda *the contested processes by which labor is disembedded from and reembedded within the social.* Not only would this be in line with the spirit of *The Great Transformation*, but it would allow economic sociology to bring its unique theoretical toolkit to bear upon contemporary debates surrounding the retreat of regulated capitalism, the revival of market fundamentalism, and the future of work.

What distinguishes the great transformation as a turning point in the history of our species, Polanyi argued, was that for the first time market principles were used on a grand scale to regulate the exchange of land (via rents), money (via interest), and labor (via wages). The commodification of the third member of this trio was especially jarring. No longer was work to be imagined as a duty for God, a gift to nature, aid for a companion, or an obligation to one's brethren. Your labor was now a commodity; you sold it on the open market; and you did so because it was the only way to acquire the means for your survival.

Thus was established the fulcrum on which the lever of history subsequently pivots. Apostles of the market push to disembed labor from traditional constraints, while advocates of society seek to reembed it in properly human values. Acts such as the English enclosure movement, which privatized grazing lands that had long been commonly held and thereby forced the peasantry into the urban labor market, were an opening salvo of this struggle. In turn, the multiple social movements that emerged independently and spontaneously in the late nineteenth and early twentieth centuries as a response had as their common thread a desire to protect communities from the injurious effects of ceaseless commodification. The success of the trade union movement, the elaboration of regulations to protect workers, and the establishment of basic social welfare protections, in this framework, were common elements of a larger "counter-movement" by society against the market.

Can we view the broad trajectory of the capitalist world since the 1980s as a new wave of disembedding the economic from the social? As a counter-counter-movement? Terms such as neoliberalism – denoting a rebirth of the market-based credo originally expounded by classic liberalists – suggest so. The more interesting question is how the current wave of marketization differs from the original. Is it merely a case of the pendulum swinging back – of a second coming of the same rough beast, to paraphrase Yeats – or is there something qualitatively different about the great transformation of our time?

It is beyond the scope of the present volume to answer such questions in a definitive manner. But we can point to two broad developments – in *globalization* and *governance* – and discuss their implications for the fate and place of labor. To take the first of these, we have what is known in general parlance as globalization – the sense that our world is more interconnected today than it has ever been before (Castells 1996). Of course the newness of globalization should not be overstated (Brady et al. 2005; Guillen 2001). The original great transformation was driven in large part by the imperatives of administering the vast colonial empires of England and other European states. Some statistics suggest that intranational, as opposed to international, trade continues to constitute the bulk of economic exchange well into the twenty-first century (Fligstein 2001a).

Nonetheless, it can be argued that key advances in communication and transportation technologies have served to connect different parts of the global economy in novel ways. Some of these are quite well known – the advent of email and ecommerce in the 1980s, for instance, along with fiber-optic data cable in the 1990s, allowed for the coordination of production and trade across vast distances (Friedman 2005). Some are less so. As Levinson (2008) points out, the standardization of container boxes during the 1960s slashed costs and transport times in the transoceanic shipping industry. It would be erroneous to argue that information technology or shipping containers *caused* the neoliberal revolution of the 1980s and 1990s, just as it would be incorrect to say that the invention of the spinning jenny caused the industrial revolution. But we are justified to say that by expanding the realm of parties with whom one can transact on a real-time basis, these technologies *enabled* an expansion of the overall market pattern.

New technologies were a necessary but not sufficient condition for globalization and neoliberalism. Their emergence coincided with a refinement of market-based methods of governance. The great transformation itself, many have argued, entailed a revolution in the ways in which individuals and states governed themselves (Collins 1980). The "traditional dispositions" (Bourdieu 1990) and "collective consciousness" (Durkheim 1997 [1893]) which had long guided action left people content to earn enough for subsistence and a bit of savings. But capitalism could only take off when people (and especially entrepreneurs) ceased "group thinking" and began to plan systematically how best to maximize their own profits. Rulers, meanwhile, had to learn to stop treating their subjects as children to be disciplined and other states as territories to be conquered. Absolutism and mercantilism were incompatible with the sensible governance of a modern market economy (Dean 2009).

As argued by political theorists such as Peter Miller and Nikolas Rose (1990), it was the development and elaboration of new technologies that facilitated governance in accord with the principles of the market. In this view, capitalist economies were long stifled by a lack of tools that could centralize information and reduce uncertainty for transacting parties. Faith, superstition, and blind obedience to tradition ruled. It was the invention of conventions of calculation and inscription (such as censuses, sample-based surveys, statistical modeling, demographics, epidemiology, etc.) that allowed populations to emerge as objects of knowledge and manipulation. Such tools then diffused into the private economy, as when government survey techniques initially intended to guide propaganda campaigns during wartime were adopted by corporate marketers to mold consumer tastes (Igo 2007). Some have even argued that these various models for tracking market transactions can become so powerful as to then influence the phenomena they purport to describe (MacKenzie and Millo 2003).

Emergent technologies of governance allow ever more minute calculations of value, across shorter time-frames, and into new inter-organizational spaces. The end result is that market logics have outpaced the ability of regulatory institutions (be they states, unions, or social movements) to rein them in (Strange 1996). Two examples can give a flavor of this. First, there is the rise of a shareholder value conception of control. Since the 1980s, we've seen an increase in the total share of capital markets under the control of institutional investors such as hedge funds, investment banks, and pension funds (Espeland and Hirsch 1990; Lazonick and O'Sullivan 2000). Individual stock-holders tend to be passive and operate with a long time-frame (e.g., by reevaluating their portfolios of holdings annually). Institutional investors, in contrast, employ professional fund managers, take a more active role in regard to the firms they invest in, and monitor share data on a real-time basis. This has had profound implications for labor (Osterman 1999). Firms increasingly redirect earnings from workers and other "stakeholders" to shareholders, and treat labor as a variable rather than a fixed cost of production (Deal and Kennedy 2000; Useem 1999).

Related are transformations in how firms manage their relationships with external suppliers – what has been called the logistics revolution. A key feature of regulated capitalism was that these relationships tended to be stable and durable, allowing knowledge, ideas, and trust to flow across organizational boundaries (Whitford and Potter 2007). But such vertical integration is now replaced by a new technology of organization governance: intensive supply chain management. Managers utilize powers of IT such as inventory tracking and sales analyses to collect information, evaluate constantly the performance of current trading partners, and monitor the larger market of potential suppliers (Wathne and Heide 2004). Thus, just as shareholders increasingly govern firms in line with a short-term market logic, firms govern suppliers by squeezing from them maximum value at minimum cost. Not embedded exchange but arm's-length transacting is the order of the day.

So let us reflect upon how these broad developments in globalization and governance can explain the dual trends discussed throughout this volume, namely the marketization of employment and the decline of organized labor. It may be helpful to return to the threefold bases of worker power introduced in the previous chapter. Workplace power, or the leverage that derives from one's position in the overall production process (and which can be adequately operationalized as the effect upon an employer of a coordinated work stoppage at a given work site), has eroded insofar as the elaboration and diversification of supply chains have fragmented production processes and insulated firms from disruptions at any one point in the chain. Under Fordism, a company generally had three choices if some subset of employees struck: it could meet their demands; it could bargain in the hope of obtaining a mutually satisfactory settlement; or it could seek victory by waiting the strikers out, bringing in replacement workers ("scabs"), or violently suppressing the entire endeavor.[1] The agile "network firm" of today, however, should it discover that employees at a supplier firm are striking, has the option to scan the supplier market and quickly negotiate a new procurement agreement.

This latter scenario may seem oversimplified – surely it cannot be so quick and easy for firms to establish new supplier relationships and scale up production accordingly? And true, the process can never be entirely frictionless or free of search costs. Nonetheless, enough data suggest that the supplier marketplace, especially in East Asia, has matured to a degree undreamed of by the large, vertically integrated firm of yesteryear. Consider the following anecdote (Duhigg and Bradsher 2012) recounting the decision by Apple Inc. to shift production of its cellular phone away from its own suppliers in California:

> One former [Apple] executive described how the company relied upon a Chinese factory to revamp iPhone manufacturing just weeks before the device was due on shelves. Apple had redesigned the iPhone's screen at the last minute, forcing an assembly line overhaul. New screens began arriving at the plant near midnight.
>
> A foreman immediately roused 8,000 workers inside the company's dormitories, according to the executive. Each employee was given a biscuit and a cup of tea, guided to a workstation and within half an hour started a 12-hour shift fitting glass screens into beveled frames. Within 96 hours, the plant was producing over 10,000 iPhones a day.
>
> "The speed and flexibility is breathtaking," the executive said. "There's no American plant that can match that."

To the extent that such supply chains continue to develop, the workplace power of workers should decline accordingly.

Continued automation and changes in the occupational structure are further undermining workplace power. Machinery and technology obviate the need for human labor in the manufacturing sector, resulting in a transition to an economy centered upon service work as the main source of employment. So the question becomes whether service jobs offer, on average, more or less workplace power than do manufacturing jobs. The evidence here is somewhat mixed. On one side are labor optimists who posit that service jobs – particularly those known as "interpersonal services"

– are more likely to be "locationally fixed" (to coin a phrase). Can you outsource the labor of your psychotherapist? Can a taxi driver be offshored? To the extent that the answer is no, workers in these occupations would seem to be immune from the sort of supply-chain leveraging that displaced the manufacture of iPhones from California to China. But the counterargument from labor pessi-mists (or, one might say, realists) is that service industries are not nearly as integrated as are manufacturing industries. A strike at a key part supplier within General Motors could and did cripple the company; a strike at a single McDonald's is unlikely to register as even a blip on the corporate radar, insofar as individual franchises are disconnected from one another.

What about the effects of globalization and neoliberal govern-ance upon workers' marketplace power – that is, their ability to control the supply of labor for their field? Professional groups cer-tainly remain powerful actors of world society (Meyer et al. 1997), and especially those based in the global North, who increasingly impose their concepts and theories upon those in the global South (Babb 2004). But the capacity of the average worker to restrict her participation in the labor market is being eroded by the dis-mantling of the welfare state. As they reduce benefits and restrict the boundaries of eligibility for public assistance, states force ever larger swaths of people into the labor market (Blau 2001). The effect is to crowd existing fields and to weaken the bargaining power of incumbent workers. While this has long been a feature of British and American governance (Esping-Andersen 1990), one of the key fallouts of the current recession has been a push for auster-ity across the societies of Europe. Deficit reduction entails fewer social services, which should, all else being equal, embolden firms and enfeeble labor.

But other conditions are not being held constant, for we are simultaneously witnessing an assault upon the third pillar of worker strength: their associational power – that is, their very capacity to form and sustain groups. This reflects a paradigm shift in state policy. In many cases, the right to unionize is removed from entire categories of people – such as employees of the state or those who supervise others in the course of their jobs. In others, obstacles to association are allowed to proliferate. Consider the inability – or perhaps unwillingness – of governments to regulate the anti-union tactics of private firms, a field of action that has developed in recent decades to a high degree of sophistication. In a study of organizing campaigns across US workplaces, Bronfenbrenner (2009) found a startlingly high number of improper, and at times illegal, maneuvers by employers to forestall unionization and thus deprive workers of a fundamental human right. Among these were the following:

- In nine out of ten union campaigns, employers held mandatory meetings in which employees were forced to listen to anti-union speeches and presentations. The majority of employers also required their front-line managers to communicate anti-union messages to workers.
- Seventy-five percent of the time, firms hired outside consultants to coordinate propaganda campaigns.
- In one-third of organizing drives, at least one worker was illegally dismissed because of his or her interest in or involvement with the union.

Given such intense and coordinated opposition, is it any surprise that workers' organizations are on the decline across much of the industrialized, capitalist world? Is it puzzling that market-based principles increasingly govern the employment exchange, or, to state this same idea in our chosen terminology, that employment has been disembedded from the social? Perhaps the more salient question is whether workers and those who advocate for them are attempting to reembed labor in the social, and, if so, how they are going about doing it and with what prospects of success.

Reactions to the marketization of human labor need not take a single form, Polanyi argued in *The Great Transformation*. The New Deal in the United States, the rise of fascism in Italy, and the success of socialism in Russia, though they differed profoundly in initial form and eventual fate, all represented an attempt by publics to counteract the ascendant market logic. The model represented by the first of this trio – the social welfare state – proved more durable than the others. But there is no reason to think that this is an exhaustive list. Just as the current wave of marketization differs from previous ones, we would expect that the "counter-movements" of today and the future will take unique forms as well (Davis and McAdam 2000). To conclude this book I would like to lay out three possible counter-movement trajectories.

One is a revival of what is known in the United States as the Great Society. This is a system of social welfare and worker protections that functions, intentionally or otherwise, to constrain the marketization of the employment relation. It also recognizes the voice of labor unions in terms of industrial governance. Europe's "Nordic states" (consisting of Norway, Sweden, Denmark, Finland, and the Netherlands) are oftentimes held up as exemplars of such a system, though even these nations have seen a retrenchment of basic social-democratic principles in recent years. As of this writing, it must be admitted that this path looks to be an uncertain one, if only because the ongoing fiscal crises across industrialized democracies have generated a new common sense that what is needed is austerity and flexibility. Risk is continuously being shifted from states and firms to individuals and families. Labor unions and those who advocate for workers, in turn, can but fight rearguard actions to preserve existing entitlements and prevent further erosion of the social welfare system.

A second possibility is that certain key principles of the Great Society model can be modified and extended to fit the contours of the new neoliberal order. Apparatuses of governance, this argument goes, must be retrofitted to take account of the fact that capital is increasingly untethered from specific industries, regions, and nations. Fewer and fewer people should expect a job with a single company over the course of a lifetime. But rather than a free-for-all space of workers constantly seeking firms and firms constantly seeking workers, the possibility is raised of employees tying themselves to particular crafts while the state provides a broad social safety net. Often labeled "flexicurity," it represents a system in which companies have latitude to increase or decrease the size of their workforces in response to the business cycle, while workers, even though they do not have job security, do have broad material security. In its most optimistic formulations, the flexicurity thesis posits that these more open-ended work arrangements will beget a more decentralized practice of citizenship and a more encompassing notion of work itself as a form of "civic labor" (Beck 2000).

Yet a third path is for workers and unions to forge new connections with the various collective actors known as the "new social movements." At the same time that organized labor has seen its influence and membership wane, a panoply of other movements have arisen which mobilize actors based upon "identities rooted in the society outside the workplace [such as] sex, race, ethnicity, age, disability, and sexual orientation" (Piore and Safford 2006: 299). It is interesting to consider the precise stance that such groups may take toward the notion of embeddedness. In many instances, marketization can be beneficial for minorities and the vulnerable. Under regulated capitalism, too often was a worker defined as an able-bodied, heterosexual white male who reproduced his position through nepotism and "old boys' networks," while all others were consigned to separate and unequal spheres such as unpaid housework, the black market, or informal labor. Movements of the latter in turn often called for an expansion of the market logic and a restriction upon informal social processes. What was embeddedness for one person was discrimination for another.

This is not to deny that organized labor can forge associational power with new social movements, but rather to emphasize that such collaborations will necessitate a reflexive understanding of how market logics can both exacerbate and constrain inequalities. It is impossible to predict what form broad movements for de-marketization will take. The future, we might say, is a blank canvas and the sociologist can only speculate as to how it will be painted. Yet, as Beck (2000: 3) argues, one thing seems certain: "The picture of society ... [will] change dramatically under the influence of a political economy of insecurity." Policy-makers and publics, employees and employers, job-seekers and job-shirkers, all will struggle with the question of how to manage the fictitious commodity that is labor.

Notes

Chapter 2 The Great Transformation of Work

1 The interested reader should refer to Polanyi's opus as well as the work of Clark (2008), de Vries (2008), and Hobsbawm (1999 [1968]).
2 Some scholars argue that this transformation was not as radical as is commonly supposed. See, for instance, Wallerstein (2011).
3 This is not to say that gift economies are devoid of power and inequality. In fact, they may be especially good at masking relations of exploitation, a subject to be explored in chapter 6.

Chapter 3 Classifying Labor

1 For a summary of current debates on the cultural versus biological bases of human classification systems, see Martin (2001).
2 Notably, Marx labeled most of the groups discussed so far – prostitutes, criminals, and so on – as a dangerous underclass, or *lumpenproletariat*.
3 International differences do exist in the extent to which the typical person believes luck, connections, ability, and work ethic affect one's chances of success.

Chapter 6 Controlling Labor

1 To avoid any confusion, note that game-based models of labor control discussed herein are not synonymous with game theory as it is used in microeconomics.
2 For an original sociological formulation, see Gouldner (1960).

Notes

Chapter 8 Conclusion: What Good is Embeddedness?

1 Of course, the larger political and legal contexts influence the decision-making process. Are sympathy strikes prohibited? Can employers hire scabs? Does the state support collective bargaining? Can the police be called upon to crush the strike?

References

Abbott, Andrew. 1988. *The System of Professions: An Essay on the Division of Expert Labor*. Chicago: University of Chicago Press.

Akerlof, George A. 1970. "The Market for 'Lemons': Quality Uncertainty and the Market Mechanism." *The Quarterly Journal of Economics* 84: 488–50.

Akerlof, George A. 1982. "Labor Contracts as Partial Gift Exchange." *The Quarterly Journal of Economics* 97(4): 543–69.

Allen, Douglas W. 2011. *The Institutional Revolution: Measurement and the Economic Emergence of the Modern World*. Chicago: University of Chicago Press.

Amenta, Edwin. 2000. *Bold Relief: Institutional Politics and the Origins of Modern American Social Policy*. Princeton, NJ: Princeton University Press.

Amenta, Edwin. 2007. *Professor Baseball: Searching for Redemption and the Perfect Lineup on the Softball Diamonds of Central Park*. Chicago: University of Chicago Press.

Anteby, Michel. 2008. *Moral Gray Zones: Side Productions, Identity, and Regulation in an Aeronautic Plant*. Princeton, NJ: Princeton University Press.

Aoki, Masahiko, Gregory Jackson, and Hideaki Miyajima. 2007. *Corporate Governance in Japan: Institutional Change and Organizational Diversity*. New York: Oxford University Press.

Aronowitz, Stanley. 1973. *False Promises: The Shaping of American Working Class Consciousness*. New York: McGraw Hill.

Arrighi, Giovanni. 2009. *Adam Smith in Beijing: Lineages of the 21st Century*. London: Verso.

Arrow, Kenneth J. 1966. "Exposition of the Theory of Choice under Uncertainty." *Synthese* 16: 253–69.

Arrow, Kenneth J. 1998. "What Has Economics to Say about Racial Discrimination?" *The Journal of Economic Perspectives* 12(2): 91–100.

Aubenas, Florence. 2011. *The Night Cleaner*. Cambridge, UK: Polity.

References

Babb, Sarah. 2004. *Managing Mexico: Economists from Nationalism to Neoliberalism*. Princeton, NJ: Princeton University Press.

Baccaro, Lucio, and Chris Howell. 2011. "A Common Neoliberal Trajectory: The Transformation of Industrial Relations in Advanced Capitalism." *Politics and Society* 39(4): 521–63.

Bandelj, Nina. 2009a. "The Global Economy as Instituted Process: The Case of Central and Eastern Europe." *American Sociological Review* 74(1): 128–49.

Bandelj, Nina, ed. 2009b. *Economic Sociology of Work*. Bingley, UK: Emerald Group.

Barber, Bernard. 1995. "All Economies Are 'Embedded': The Career of a Concept, and Beyond." *Social Research* 62: 388–413.

Barley, Stephen R., and Gideon Kunda. 1992. "Design and Devotion: Surges of Rational and Normative Ideologies of Control in Managerial Discourse." *Administrative Science Quarterly* 37(3): 363–99.

Baron, James N., Frank R. Dobbin, and P. Devereaux Jennings. 1986. "War and Peace: The Evolution of Modern Personnel Administration in US Industry." *American Journal of Sociology* 92(2): 350–83.

Bartley, Tim. 2003. "Certifying Forests and Factories: States, Social Movements, the Rise of Private Regulation in the Apparel and Forest Products Fields." *Politics and Society* 31: 433–64.

Bearman, Peter. 2005. *Doormen*. Chicago: University of Chicago Press.

Beauvoir, Simone de. 2011 [1949]. *The Second Sex*, trans. Constance Borde and Sheila Malovany-Chevallier. New York: Vintage.

Bebchuk, Lucian, and Jesse Fried. 2004. *Pay without Performance: The Unfulfilled Promise of Executive Compensation*. Cambridge, MA: Harvard University Press.

Beck, Ulrich. 2000. *The Brave New World of Work*, trans. Patrick Camiller. Cambridge, UK: Polity.

Becker, Gary S. 1971. *The Economics of Discrimination*. 2nd edn. Chicago: University of Chicago Press.

Becker, Howard S. 1997 [1963]. *Outsiders: Studies in the Sociology of Deviance*. New York: Free Press.

Beckert, Jens. 2002. *Beyond the Market: The Social Foundations of Economic Efficiency*, trans. Barbara Harshav. Princeton, NJ: Princeton University Press.

Beckert, Jens, and Patrik Aspers, eds. 2011. *The Worth of Goods: Valuation and Pricing in the Economy*. New York: Oxford University Press.

Bendix, Reinhard. 1956. *Work and Authority in Industry: Managerial Ideologies in the Course of Industrialization*. New Brunswick, NJ: Transaction Publishers.

Benford, Robert D., and David A. Snow. 2000. "Framing Processes and Social Movements: An Overview and Assessment." *Annual Review of Sociology* 26: 611–39.

Berggren, Christian. 1994. *The Volvo Experience: Alternatives to Lean Production in the Swedish Auto Industry*. London: Palgrave Macmillan.

References

Bernstein, Elizabeth. 2007. *Temporarily Yours: Intimacy, Authenticity, and the Commerce of Sex*. Chicago: University of Chicago Press.

Biernacki, Richard. 1995. *The Fabrication of Labor: Germany and Britain, 1640–1914*. Berkeley: University of California Press.

Biggart, Nicole Woolsey, and Mauro F. Guillén. 1999. "Developing Difference: Social Organization and the Rise of the Auto Industries of South Korea, Taiwan, Spain, and Argentina." *American Sociological Review* 64(5): 722–47.

Blau, Joel. 2001. *Illusions of Prosperity: America's Working Families in an Age of Economic Insecurity*. New York: Oxford University Press.

Blinder, Alan S. 2006. "Offshoring: The Next Industrial Revolution?" *Foreign Affairs* 85(2): 113–28.

Bloch, Marc. 1964. *Feudal Society, Volume 1: The Growth of Ties of Dependence*. Chicago: University of Chicago Press.

Block, Fred. 1990. *Postindustrial Possibilities: A Critique of Economic Discourse*. Berkeley: University of California Press.

Block, Fred. 2003. "Karl Polanyi and the Writing of *The Great Transformation*." *Theory and Society* 32(3): 275–306.

Bloemraad, Irene. 2006. *Becoming a Citizen: Incorporating Immigrants and Refugees in the United States and Canada*. Berkeley: University of California Press.

Boltanski, Luc, and Eve Chiapello. 2005. *The New Spirit of Capitalism*, trans. Gregory Elliott. London: Verso.

Boltanski, Luc, and Laurent Thévenot. 2006. *On Justification: Economies of Worth*, trans. Catherine Porter. Princeton, NJ: Princeton University Press.

Bonacich, Edna, and Richard Appelbaum. 2000. *Behind the Label: Inequality in the Los Angeles Apparel Industry*. Berkeley: University of California Press.

Bonnell, Rick. 2011. "NBA Lockout Opens Door for Stephen Curry's Education." *Charlotte Observer*, October 2. http://www.charlotteobserver.com/2011/10/02/2656635/stephen-curry-at-davidson.html (accessed July 31, 2012).

Bourdieu, Pierre. 1979. *Algeria 1960*, trans. Richard Nice. Cambridge, UK: Cambridge University Press.

Bourdieu, Pierre. 1985. "The Genesis of the Concepts Habitus and Field." *Sociocriticism* 2 (2): 11–24.

Bourdieu, Pierre. 1990. *The Logic of Practice*, trans. Richard Nice. Stanford, CA: Stanford University Press.

Bourdieu, Pierre. 1998. *The State Nobility: Elite Schools in the Field of Power*, trans. Lauretta C. Clough. Stanford, CA: Stanford University Press.

Bourdieu, Pierre. 1999 [1991]. *Language and Symbolic Power*, trans. Gino Raymond and Matthew Adamson. Cambridge, MA: Harvard University Press.

Bourdieu, Pierre. 2001. *Masculine Domination*, trans. Richard Nice. Cambridge, UK: Polity.

References

Bourdieu, Pierre. 2004. "From the King's House to the Reason of State: A Model of the Genesis of the Bureaucratic Field." *Constellations* 11(1): 16–36.

Bourdieu, Pierre. 2005. *The Social Structures of the Economy*, trans. Chris Turner. Cambridge, UK: Polity.

Bourdieu, Pierre, and Jean-Claude Passeron. 1977. *Reproduction in Education, Society and Culture*, trans. Richard Nice. London: Sage.

Bowles, Hannah Riley, and Kathleen L. McGinn. 2008. "Untapped Potential in the Study of Negotiation and Gender Inequality in Organizations." *The Academy of Management Annals* 2(1): 99–132.

Brady, David, Jason Beckfield, and Martin Seeleib-Kaiser. 2005. "Economic Globalization and the Welfare State in Affluent Democracies, 1975–2001." *American Sociological Review* 70(6): 921–48.

Bramel, Dana, and Ronald Friend. 1981. "Hawthorne, the Myth of the Docile Worker, and Class Bias in Psychology." *American Psychologist* 36(8): 867–78.

Braverman, Harry. 1974. *Labor and Monopoly Capital: The Degradation of Work in the Twentieth Century*. New York: Monthly Review Press.

Brint, Steven. 1996. *In an Age of Experts: The Changing Role of Professionals in Politics and Public Life*. Princeton, NJ: Princeton University Press.

Bronfenbrenner, Kate. 2009. *No Holds Barred: The Intensification of Employer Opposition to Organizing*. Washington, DC: Economic Policy Institute.

Brown, Robbie, and Kim Severson. 2011. "Enlisting Prison Labor to Close Budget Gaps." *The New York Times*, February 24, sec. US. http://www.nytimes.com/2011/02/25/us/25inmates.html?pagewanted=all (accessed July 31, 2012).

Burawoy, Michael. 1972. *The Colour of Class on the Copper Mines: From African Advancement to Zambianization*. Manchester: Manchester University Press.

Burawoy, Michael. 1979a. *Manufacturing Consent*. Chicago: University of Chicago Press.

Burawoy, Michael. 1979b. "The Anthropology of Industrial Work." *Annual Review of Anthropology* 8(1): 231–66.

Burawoy, Michael. 1985. *The Politics of Production: Factory Regimes under Capitalism and Socialism*. London: Verso.

Burawoy, Michael, and János Lukács. 1985. "Mythologies of Work: A Comparison of Firms in State Socialism and Advanced Capitalism." *American Sociological Review* 50(6): 723–37.

Burke, Jason. 2011. "Chained to Their Desks: Prisoners Will Staff Call Centre within Indian Jail." *The Guardian*, February 1. http://www.guardian.co.uk/world/2011/feb/01/call-centre-inside-indian-jail (accessed July 31, 2012).

Callon, Michel, Cécile Méadel, and Vololona Rabeharisoa. 2002. "The Economy of Qualities." *Economy and Society* 31(2): 194–217.

Campbell, John L., and Leon N. Lindberg. 1990. "Property Rights and the

References

Organization of Economic Activity by the State." *American Sociological Review* 55(5): 634–47.

Carruthers, Bruce G., and Laura Ariovich. 2004. "The Sociology of Property Rights." *Annual Review of Sociology* 30: 23–46.

Castells, Manuel. 1996. *The Rise of the Network Society: The Information Age: Economy, Society, and Culture*. Malden, MA: John Wiley & Sons.

Chambliss, Daniel F. 1996. *Beyond Caring: Hospitals, Nurses, and the Social Organization of Ethics*. Chicago: University of Chicago Press.

Chandler, Alfred D., Jr. 1977. *The Visible Hand: The Managerial Revolution in American Business*. Cambridge, MA: Harvard University Press.

Chandler, Alfred D., Jr. 1984. "The Emergence of Managerial Capitalism." *The Business History Review* 58(4): 473–503.

Chen, Katherine K. 2009. *Enabling Creative Chaos: The Organization behind the Burning Man Event*. Chicago: University of Chicago Press.

Chun, Jennifer. 2010. *Organizing at the Margins: The Symbolic Politics of Labor in South Korea and the United States*. Ithaca, NY: Cornell University Press.

Clark, Gregory. 2008. *A Farewell to Alms: A Brief Economic History of the World*. Princeton, NJ: Princeton University Press.

Clawson, Dan. 2003. *The Next Upsurge: Labor and the New Social Movements*. Ithaca, NY: Cornell University Press.

Clinton, Bill. 2006. "How We Ended Welfare, Together." *The New York Times*, August 22, sec. Opinion. http://www.nytimes.com/2006/08/22/opinion/22clinton.html (accessed July 31, 2012).

Coase, R. H. 1992. "The Institutional Structure of Production." *The American Economic Review* 82(4): 713–19.

Collins, Jane Lou, and Victoria Mayer. 2010. *Both Hands Tied: Welfare Reform and the Race to the Bottom in the Low-wage Labor Market*. Chicago: University of Chicago Press.

Collins, Randall. 1980. "Weber's Last Theory of Capitalism: A Systematization." *American Sociological Review* 45(6): 925–42.

Cornwell, Benjamin, and Jill Ann Harrison. 2004. "Union Members and Voluntary Associations: Membership Overlap as a Case of Organizational Embeddedness." *American Sociological Review* 69(6): 862–81.

Costa, Dora L. 1998. *The Evolution of Retirement: An American Economic History, 1880–1990*. Chicago: University of Chicago Press.

Crittenden, Ann. 2001. *The Price of Motherhood: Why the Most Important Job in the World is Still the Least Valued*. New York: Metropolitan Books.

Crozier, Michel. 1964. *The Bureaucratic Phenomenon*. Chicago: University of Chicago Press.

Cutler, Jonathan. 2004. *Labor's Time: Shorter Hours, the UAW, and the Struggle for American Unionism*. Philadelphia, PA: Temple University Press.

Dalton, Melville. 1948. "The Industrial 'Rate-Buster': A Characterization." *Applied Anthropology* 7(1): 5–18.

References

Darr, Asaf. 2003. "Gifting Practices and Interorganizational Relations: Constructing Obligation Networks in the Electronics Sector." *Sociological Forum* 18(1): 31–51.

Davis, Fred. 1959. "The Cabdriver and His Fare: Facets of a Fleeting Relationship." *American Journal of Sociology* 65(2): 158–65.

Davis, Gerald, and Douglas McAdam. 2000. "Corporations, Classes, and Social Movement after Managerialism." In *Research in Organizational Behavior*, ed. Barry M. Staw and Robert I. Sutton. Greenwich, CT: JAI Press, 195–238.

de Vries, Jan. 2008. *The Industrious Revolution: Consumer Behavior and the Household Economy, 1650 to the Present*. New York: Cambridge University Press.

Deal, Terrence E., and Allan A. Kennedy. 2000. *The New Corporate Cultures: Revitalizing the Workplace after Downsizing, Mergers, and Reengineering*. Cambridge, MA: Perseus Publishing.

Dean, Jason. 2010. "Suicides Spark Inquiries." *Wall Street Journal*, May 27, sec. Technology. http://online.wsj.com/article/SB10001424052748704026204575 267603576594936.html (accessed July 31, 2012).

Dean, Mitchell. 2009. *Governmentality: Power and Rule in Modern Society*. Thousand Oaks, CA: Sage Publications.

Desai, Meghnad. 2004. *Marx's Revenge: The Resurgence of Capitalism and the Death of Statist Socialism*. London: Verso.

Desmond, Matthew. 2009. *On the Fireline: Living and Dying with Wildland Firefighters*. Chicago: University of Chicago Press.

DiMaggio, Paul, ed. 2003. *The Twenty-First-Century Firm: Changing Economic Organization in International Perspective*. Princeton, NJ: Princeton University Press.

Dixon, Marc, Vincent J. Roscigno, and Randy Hodson. 2004. "Unions, Solidarity, and Striking." *Social Forces* 83(1): 3–33.

Dobbin, Frank. 1997. *Forging Industrial Policy: The United States, Britain, and France in the Railway Age*. New York: Cambridge University Press.

Dobbin, Frank. 2011. *Inventing Equal Opportunity*. Princeton, NJ: Princeton University Press.

Dobbin, Frank, and Timothy J. Dowd. 2000. "The Market That Antitrust Built: Public Policy, Private Coercion, and Railroad Acquisitions, 1825 to 1922." *American Sociological Review* 65(5): 631–57.

Dore, Ronald. 1973. *British Factory–Japanese Factory: The Origins of National Diversity in Industrial Relations*. Berkeley: University of California Press.

Duhigg, Charles, and Keith Bradsher. 2012. "How the US Lost Out on iPhone Work." *The New York Times*, January 21, sec. Business Day. http://www. nytimes.com/2012/01/22/business/apple-america-and-a-squeezed-middle-class. html?pagewanted=all (accessed July 31, 2012).

Durkheim, Émile. 1997 [1893]. *The Division of Labor in Society*, trans. W. D. Halls. New York: Free Press.

References

Durkheim, Émile, and Marcel Mauss. 1963 [1903]. *Primitive Classification*, trans. Rodney Needham. Chicago: University of Chicago Press.

Emerson, Ralph Waldo. 2010 [1841]. *Essays: First and Second Series*. Stillwell, KS: CreateSpace.

Espeland, Wendy Nelson, and Paul M. Hirsch. 1990. "Ownership Changes, Accounting Practice and the Redefinition of the Corporation." *Accounting, Organizations and Society* 15(1–2): 77–96.

Espeland, Wendy Nelson, and Mitchell L. Stevens. 1998. "Commensuration as a Social Process." *Annual Review of Sociology* 24: 313–43.

Esping-Andersen, Gosta. 1990. *The Three Worlds of Welfare Capitalism*. Princeton, NJ: Princeton University Press.

Evans, Peter B. 1995. *Embedded Autonomy: States and Industrial Transformation*. Princeton, NJ: Princeton University Press.

Evans, Rhonda, and Tamara Kay. 2008. "How Environmentalists Greened Trade Policy." *American Sociological Review* 73(6): 970–91.

Eyal, Gil, and Larissa Buchholz. 2010. "From the Sociology of Intellectuals to the Sociology of Interventions." *Annual Review of Sociology* 36: 117–37.

Fantasia, Rick. 1988. *Cultures of Solidarity: Consciousness, Action, and Contemporary American Workers*. Berkeley: University of California Press.

Fligstein, Neil. 1993. *The Transformation of Corporate Control*. Cambridge, MA: Harvard University Press.

Fligstein, Neil. 1996. "Markets as Politics: A Political-Cultural Approach to Market Institutions." *American Sociological Review* 61: 656–73.

Fligstein, Neil. 2001a. *The Architecture of Markets: An Economic Sociology of Twenty-First-Century Capitalist Societies*. Princeton, NJ: Princeton University Press.

Fligstein, Neil. 2001b. "Social Skill and the Theory of Fields." *Sociological Theory* 19(2): 105–25.

Fligstein, Neil, and Roberto M. Fernandez. 1988. "Worker Power, Firm Power, and the Structure of Labor Markets." *The Sociological Quarterly* 29(1): 5–28.

Fligstein, Neil and Doug McAdam. 2012. *A Theory of Fields*. New York: Oxford University Press.

Foucault, Michel. 1995 [1975]. *Discipline and Punish: The Birth of the Prison*, trans. Alan Sheridan. 2nd edn. New York: Vintage.

Foucault, Michel. 1980. *Power/Knowledge: Selected Interviews and Other Writings, 1972–1977*, ed. Colin Gordon. New York: Vintage.

Fourcade, Marion. 2011. "Price and Prejudice: On Economics and the Enchantment (or Disenchantment) of Nature." In *The Worth of Goods: Valuation and Pricing in the Economy*, ed. Jens Beckert and Patrick Aspers. New York: Oxford University Press, 41–62.

Fourcade, Marion, and Kieran Healy. 2007. "Moral Views of Market Society." *Annual Review of Sociology* 33: 285–311.

Frank, Robert H., and Philip J. Cook. 1996. *The Winner-Take-All Society:*

References

Why the Few at the Top Get So Much More Than the Rest of Us. New York: Penguin.

Fredrickson, George M. 1982. *White Supremacy: A Comparative Study of American and South African History.* New York: Oxford University Press.

Friedman, Andy. 1977. "Responsible Autonomy versus Direct Control over the Labour Process." *Capital & Class* 1(1): 43–57.

Friedman, Milton. 2002 [1962]. *Capitalism and Freedom.* 40th anniversary edn. Chicago: University of Chicago Press.

Friedman, Thomas L. 2005. *The World is Flat: A Brief History of the Twenty-First Century.* New York: Farrar, Straus and Giroux.

Gannon, Martin. 1974. "A Profile of the Temporary Help Industry and Its Workers." *Monthly Labor Review* 95: 44–9.

Garth, Bryant, and Joyce Sterling. 1998. "From Legal Realism to Law and Society: Reshaping Law for the Last Stages of the Social Activist State." *Law & Society Review* 32(2): 409–72.

Geertz, Clifford. 1978. "The Bazaar Economy: Information and Search in Peasant Marketing." *The American Economic Review* 68(2): 28–32.

Gerber, Theodore P., and Sin Yi Cheung. 2008. "Horizontal Stratification in Postsecondary Education: Forms, Explanations, and Implications." *Annual Review of Sociology* 34: 299–318.

Gerlach, Michael L. 1997. *Alliance Capitalism: The Social Organization of Japanese Business.* Berkeley: University of California Press.

Goffman, Alice. 2009. "On the Run: Wanted Men in a Philadelphia Ghetto." *American Sociological Review* 74(3): 339–57.

Goffman, Erving. 1961. *Asylums: Essays on the Social Situation of Mental Patients and Other Inmates.* New York: Anchor Books.

Goffman, Erving. 1963. *Stigma: Notes on the Management of Spoiled Identity.* New York: Simon and Schuster, Inc.

Gottfried, Heidi. 1991. "Mechanisms of Control in the Temporary Help Service Industry." *Sociological Forum* 6(4): 699–713.

Gouldner, Alvin W. 1960. "The Norm of Reciprocity: A Preliminary Statement." *American Sociological Review* 25(2): 161–78.

Gouldner, Alvin W. 1964. *Patterns of Industrial Bureaucracy.* New York: Free Press.

Graeber, David. 2011. *Debt: The First 5,000 Years.* New York: Melville House.

Gramsci, Antonio. 1971. *Selections from the Prison Notebooks*, ed. Quintin Hoare and Geoffrey Nowell-Smith. New York: International Publishers Co.

Granovetter, Mark S. 1973. "The Strength of Weak Ties." *American Journal of Sociology* 78(6): 1360–80.

Granovetter, Mark S. 1985. "Economic Action and Social Structure: The Problem of Embeddedness." *American Journal of Sociology* 91(3): 481–510.

Granovetter, Mark S. 1995 [1974]. *Getting a Job: A Study of Contacts and Careers.* 2nd edn. Chicago: University of Chicago Press.

References

Grant, Don, Alfonso Morales, and Jeffrey J. Sallaz. 2009. "Pathways to Meaning: A New Approach to Studying Emotions at Work." *American Journal of Sociology* 115(2): 327–64.

Greenhouse, Steven, and Karen W. Arenson. 2004. "Labor Board Says Graduate Students at Private Universities Have No Right to Unionize." *The New York Times*, July 16, sec. Education. http://www.nytimes.com/2004/07/16/education/16union.html (accessed July 31, 2012).

Guillen, Mauro F. 2001. "Is Globalization Civilizing, Destructive or Feeble? A Critique of Five Key Debates in the Social Science Literature." *Annual Review of Sociology* 27: 235–60.

Gutek, Barbara A. 1995. *The Dynamics of Service: Reflections on the Changing Nature of Customer/Provider Interactions*. San Francisco, CA: Jossey-Bass.

Hall, Peter A., and David Soskice, eds. 2001. *Varieties of Capitalism: The Institutional Foundations of Comparative Advantage*. New York: Oxford University Press.

Halliday, Terence C., and Bruce G. Carruthers. 2007. "The Recursivity of Law: Global Norm Making and National Lawmaking in the Globalization of Corporate Insolvency Regimes." *American Journal of Sociology* 112(4): 1135–202.

Hamermesh, Daniel S. 2011. *Beauty Pays: Why Attractive People are More Successful*. Princeton, NJ: Princeton University Press.

Hamilton, Gary G., and Nicole W. Biggart. 1988. "Market, Culture and Authority: A Comparative Analysis of Management and Organization in the Far East." *American Journal of Sociology* 94: S52–S94.

Harvey, David. 2007. *A Brief History of Neoliberalism*. New York: Oxford University Press.

Harvey, David. 2011. *The Enigma of Capital: And the Crises of Capitalism*. New York: Oxford University Press.

Hatton, Erin. 2011. *The Temp Economy: From Kelly Girls to Permatemps in Postwar America*. Philadelphia, PA: Temple University Press.

Hayek, F. A. 1996 [1948]. *Individualism and Economic Order*. Chicago: University of Chicago Press.

Head, Simon. 2005. *The New Ruthless Economy: Work and Power in the Digital Age*. New York: Oxford University Press.

Healy, Kieran. 2006. *Last, Best Gifts: Altruism and the Market for Human Blood and Organs*. Chicago: University of Chicago Press.

Helper, Susan. 1991. "Strategy and Irreversibility in Supplier Relations: The Case of the US Automobile Industry." *The Business History Review* 65(4): 781–824.

Hirschman, Albert O. 1968. "The Political Economy of Import-Substituting Industrialization in Latin America." *The Quarterly Journal of Economics* 82(1): 1–32.

Hirschman, Albert O. 1997 [1977]. *The Passions and the Interests: Political*

References

Arguments for Capitalism Before Its Triumph. 20th anniversary edn. Princeton, NJ: Princeton University Press.

Hobsbawm, Eric. 1999 [1968]. *Industry and Empire: The Birth of the Industrial Revolution.* New York: The New Press.

Hochschild, Arlie Russell. 1983. *The Managed Heart: Commercialization of Human Feeling.* Berkeley: University of California Press.

Hochschild, Arlie Russell, and Anne Machung. 1989. *The Second Shift.* New York: Viking.

Hodson, Randy. 2001. *Dignity at Work.* New York: Cambridge University Press.

Hsu, Greta, Michael T. Hannan, and Özgecan Koçak. 2009. "Multiple Category Memberships in Markets: An Integrative Theory and Two Empirical Tests." *American Sociological Review* 74(1): 150–69.

Hughes, Everett C. 1962. "Good People and Dirty Work." *Social Problems* 10(1): 3–11.

Human Rights Watch. 2011. *The Rehab Archipelago: Forced Labor and Other Abuses in Drug Detention Centers in Southern Vietnam.* New York: Human Rights Watch.

Igo, Sarah E. 2007. *The Averaged American: Surveys, Citizens, and the Making of a Mass Public.* Cambridge, MA: Harvard University Press.

Illich, Ivan. 2000 [1981]. *Shadow Work.* New York: Marion Boyars Publishers Ltd.

Jacoby, Sanford M. 2004 [1985]. *Employing Bureaucracy: Managers, Unions, and the Transformation of Work in the 20th Century.* Revised edn. Mahway, NJ: Psychology Press.

Jutting, Johannes P., and Juan R. de Laiglesia. 2009. *Is Informal Normal? Towards More and Better Jobs in Developing Countries.* Paris: Organization for Economic Co-operation and Development.

Kahneman, Daniel. 2011. *Thinking, Fast and Slow.* New York: Farrar, Straus and Giroux.

Kalleberg, Arne L. 2009. "Precarious Work, Insecure Workers: Employment Relations in Transition." *American Sociological Review* 74(1): 1–22.

Kant, Immanuel. 1999 [1781]. *Critique of Pure Reason*, trans. Paul Guyer and Allen W. Wood. New York: Cambridge University Press.

Kanter, Rosabeth Moss. 1993 [1977]. *Men and Women of the Corporation.* 2nd edn. New York: Basic Books.

Katznelson, Ira, and Aristide R. Zolberg, eds. 1986. *Working-Class Formation: Nineteenth-Century Patterns in Western Europe and the United States.* Princeton, NJ: Princeton University Press.

Keister, Lisa. 2000. *Chinese Business Groups: The Structure and Impact of Interfirm Relations during Economic Development.* New York: Oxford University Press.

Kenworthy, Lane. 2007. *Egalitarian Capitalism: Jobs, Incomes, and Growth in Affluent Countries.* New York: Russell Sage Foundation.

References

Khurana, Rakesh. 2002. *Searching for a Corporate Savior: The Irrational Quest for Charismatic CEOs*. Princeton, NJ: Princeton University Press.

Khurana, Rakesh. 2010. *From Higher Aims to Hired Hands: The Social Transformation of American Business Schools and the Unfulfilled Promise of Management as a Profession*. Princeton, NJ: Princeton University Press.

Krause, Monika, Mary Nolan, Michael Palm, and Andrew Ross, eds. 2008. *The University against Itself: The NYU Strike and the Future of the Academic Workplace*. Philadelphia, PA: Temple University Press.

Krippner, Greta R. 2001. "The Elusive Market: Embeddedness and the Paradigm of Economic Sociology." *Theory and Society* 30(6): 775–810.

Krugman, Paul. 1999. *The Accidental Theorist and Other Dispatches from the Dismal Science*. New York: W. W. Norton & Company.

Kube, Sebastian, Michel André Maréchal, and Clemens Puppe. 2011. "The Currency of Reciprocity – Gift-Exchange in the Workplace." *SSRN eLibrary*. http://papers.ssrn.com/sol3/papers.cfm?abstract_id=1160170 (accessed July 31, 2012).

Kunda, Gideon. 1992. *Engineering Culture: Control and Commitment in a High-Tech Corporation*. Philadelphia, PA: Temple University Press.

Kwon, Hyeok Yong, and Jonas Pontusson. 2010. "Globalization, Labour Power and Partisan Politics Revisited." *Socio-Economic Review* 8(2): 251–81.

Lahire, Bernard. 2011. *The Plural Actor*. Cambridge, UK: Polity.

Lamont, Michèle, and Virág Molnár. 2002. "The Study of Boundaries in the Social Sciences." *Annual Review of Sociology* 28: 167–95.

Lareau, Annette. 2003. *Unequal Childhoods: Class, Race, and Family Life*. Berkeley: University of California Press.

Latour, Bruno. 1988. *Science in Action: How to Follow Scientists and Engineers through Society*. Cambridge, MA: Harvard University Press.

Lazonick, William, and Mary O'Sullivan. 2000. "Maximizing Shareholder Value: A New Ideology for Corporate Governance." *Economy and Society* 29(1): 13–35.

Lee, Ching Kwan. 1998. *Gender and the South China Miracle: Two Worlds of Factory Women*. Berkeley: University of California Press.

Lee, Ching Kwan. 2007. *Against the Law: Labor Protests in China's Rustbelt and Sunbelt*. Berkeley: University of California Press.

Leidner, Robin. 1993. *Fast Food, Fast Talk: Service Work and the Routinization of Everyday Life*. Berkeley: University of California Press.

Lévi-Strauss, Claude. 1992 [1955]. *Tristes Tropiques*, trans. John Weightman and Doreen Weightman. New York: Penguin.

Levinson, Marc. 2008. *The Box: How the Shipping Container Made the World Smaller and the World Economy Bigger*. Princeton, NJ: Princeton University Press.

Lewis, Michael. 2003. *Moneyball: The Art of Winning an Unfair Game*. New York: W. W. Norton & Company.

References

Lichtenstein, Nelson. 1997. *Walter Reuther: The Most Dangerous Man in Detroit*. Champaign: University of Illinois Press.

Lichtenstein, Nelson. 2009. *The Retail Revolution: How Wal-Mart Created a Brave New World of Business*. New York: Metropolitan Books.

Light, Ivan. 1984. "Immigrant and Ethnic Enterprise in North America." *Ethnic and Racial Studies* 7(2): 195–216.

Linder, Marc, and Ingrid Nygaard. 1998. *Void Where Prohibited: Rest Breaks and the Right to Urinate on Company Time*. Ithaca, NY: Cornell University Press.

Lipset, Seymour Martin, Noah Meltz, Rafael Gomez, and Ivan Katchanovski. 2004. *The Paradox of American Unionism: Why Americans Like Unions More Than Canadians Do, but Join Much Less*. Ithaca, NY: Cornell University Press.

Lopez, Steven Henry. 2004. *Reorganizing the Rust Belt: An Inside Study of the American Labor Movement*. Berkeley: University of California Press.

Lopez, Steven Henry. 2006. "Emotional Labor and Organized Emotional Care." *Work and Occupations* 33(2): 133–60.

Luo, Michael. 2009. "'Whitening' the Résumé." *The New York Times*, December 5, sec. Week in Review. http://www.nytimes.com/2009/12/06/weekinreview/06Luo.html (accessed July 31, 2012).

Macaulay, Stewart. 1963. "Non-Contractual Relations in Business: A Preliminary Study." *American Sociological Review* 28(1): 55–67.

McKay, Steven C. 2006. *Satanic Mills or Silicon Islands? The Politics of High-Tech Production in the Philippines*. Ithaca, NY: Cornell University Press.

MacKenzie, Donald, and Yuval Millo. 2003. "Constructing a Market, Performing Theory: The Historical Sociology of a Financial Derivatives Exchange." *American Journal of Sociology* 109(1): 107–45.

Malinowski, Bronislaw. 1922. *Argonauts of the Western Pacific*. New York: Routledge.

Martin, Isaac. 2001. "Dawn of the Living Wage: The Diffusion of a Redistributive Municipal Policy." *Urban Affairs Review* 36(4): 470–96.

Martin, John Levi. 2009. *Social Structures*. Princeton, NJ: Princeton University Press.

Marx, Karl. 1978a [1932]. "The Economic and Philosophical Manuscripts of 1844." In *The Marx–Engels Reader*, ed. Robert C. Tucker. New York: W. W. Norton & Company, 66–105.

Marx, Karl. 1978b [1849]. "Wage Labor and Capital." In *The Marx–Engels Reader*, ed. Robert C. Tucker. New York: W. W. Norton & Company, 203–17.

Marx, Karl. 1993 [1894]. *Capital: A Critique of Political Economy, Vol. 3*, trans. David Fernbach. New York: Penguin Classics.

Marx, Karl, and Friedrich Engels. 1998 [1848]. *The Communist Manifesto*. New York: Signet Classics.

Maule, David. 2008. *Inventions That Changed the World*. Harlow, UK: Penguin.

References

Mauss, Marcel. 1990 [1923]. *The Gift: The Form and Reason for Exchange in Archaic Societies*, trans. W. D. Hallas. New York: Norton.

Mead, Margaret. 2001 [1928]. *Coming of Age in Samoa: A Psychological Study of Primitive Youth for Western Civilisation.* New York: William Morrow Paperbacks.

Mears, Ashley. 2011. *Pricing Beauty: The Making of a Fashion Model.* Berkeley: University of California Press.

Meyer, John W., Francisco Ramirez, and Yasemin Soysal. 1992. "World Expansion of Mass Education: 1870–1970." *Sociology of Education* 65(2): 128–49.

Meyer, John W., John Boli, George M. Thomas, and Francisco O. Ramirez. 1997. "World Society and the Nation-State." *American Journal of Sociology* 103(1): 144–181.

Michels, Robert. 2012 [1911]. *Political Parties: A Sociological Study of the Oligarchical Tendencies of Modern Democracy.* New York: Free Press.

Milkman, Ruth. 1997. *Farewell to the Factory.* Berkeley: University of California Press.

Milkman, Ruth. 2006. *LA Story: Immigrant Workers and the Future of the US Labor Movement.* New York: Russell Sage Foundation Publications.

Miller, Peter, and Nikolas Rose. 1990. "Governing Economic Life." *Economy and Society* 19(1): 1–31.

Mills, C. Wright. 2000 [1959]. *The Sociological Imagination.* 40th anniversary edn. New York: Oxford University Press.

Mishel, Lawrence, Jared Bernstein, and Heidi Shierholz. 2009. *The State of Working America, 2008/2009.* Ithaca, NY: Cornell University Press.

Mizruchi, Mark S. 1992. *The Structure of Corporate Political Action: Interfirm Relations and Their Consequences.* Cambridge, MA: Harvard University Press.

Moretti, Enrico. 2012. *The New Geography of Jobs.* New York: Houghton Mifflin Harcourt.

Moss, Philip I., and Chris Tilly. 2001. *Stories Employers Tell: Race, Skill, and Hiring in America.* New York: Russell Sage Foundation.

Murray, R. Emmett. 2010. *The Lexicon of Labor.* New York: The New Press.

Navis, Chad, and Mary Ann Glynn. 2010. "How New Market Categories Emerge: Temporal Dynamics of Legitimacy, Identity, and Entrepreneurship in Satellite Radio, 1990–2005." *Administrative Science Quarterly* 55(3): 439–71.

Nee, Victor. 1998. "Norms and Networks in Economic and Organizational Performance." *The American Economic Review* 88(2): 85–9.

North, Douglass C. 1990. *Institutions, Institutional Change and Economic Performance.* New York: Cambridge University Press.

North, Douglass C., and Robert Paul Thomas. 1976. *The Rise of the Western World: A New Economic History.* New York: Cambridge University Press.

Oakley, Ann. 1984. *The Sociology of Housework.* New York: Wiley Blackwell.

Orloff, Ann Shola. 1993. *Politics of Pensions: A Comparative Analysis of*

References

Britain, Canada, and the United States, 1880–1940. Madison: University of Wisconsin Press.

Osterman, Paul. 1999. *Securing Prosperity.* Princeton, NJ: Princeton University Press.

Ostrom, Elinor. 1990. *Governing the Commons: The Evolution of Institutions for Collective Action.* New York: Cambridge University Press.

Pager, Devah. 2009. *Marked: Race, Crime, and Finding Work in an Era of Mass Incarceration.* Chicago: University of Chicago Press.

Paules, Greta Foff. 1991. *Dishing It Out.* Philadelphia, PA: Temple University Press.

Pedriana, Nicholas, and Robin Stryker. 2004. "The Strength of a Weak Agency: Enforcement of Title VII of the 1964 Civil Rights Act and the Expansion of State Capacity, 1965–1971." *American Journal of Sociology* 110(3): 709–60.

Perrow, Charles. 1999 [1984]. *Normal Accidents: Living with High-Risk Technologies.* Princeton, NJ: Princeton University Press.

Perrow, Charles. 2005. *Organizing America: Wealth, Power, and the Origins of Corporate Capitalism.* Princeton, NJ: Princeton University Press.

Persky, Joseph. 1995. "Retrospectives: The Ethology of *Homo Economicus.*" *The Journal of Economic Perspectives* 9(2): 221–31.

Petersen, Trond. 1992. "Payment Systems and the Structure of Inequality: Conceptual Issues and an Analysis of Salespersons in Department Stores." *American Journal of Sociology* 98(1): 67–104.

Phillips, Michael M. 2010. "Bill to Slow Overseas Hiring Debated." *Wall Street Journal,* September 26. http://online.wsj.com/article/SB100014240527487047 60704575516311129324720.html (accessed July 31, 2012).

Pierce, Jennifer L. 1996. *Gender Trials: Emotional Lives in Contemporary Law Firms.* Berkeley: University of California Press.

Pine, Joseph B., and James H. Gilmore. 1999. *The Experience Economy: Work is Theatre and Every Business a Stage.* Cambridge, MA: Harvard Business Press.

Piore, Michael J, and Sean Safford. 2006. "Changing Regimes of Workplace Governance, Shifting Axes of Social Mobilization, and the Challenge to Industrial Relations Theory." *Industrial Relations: A Journal of Economy and Society* 45(3): 299–325.

Podolny, Joel M., and Karen L. Page. 1998. "Network Forms of Organization." *Annual Review of Sociology* 24: 57–76.

Polanyi, Karl. 2001 [1944]. *The Great Transformation: The Political and Economic Origins of Our Time.* 2nd edn. Boston, MA: Beacon Press.

Polanyi, Karl, Conrad M. Arenberg, and Harry W. Pearson, eds. 1957. *Trade and Market in the Early Empires: Economies in History and Theory.* New York: Free Press.

Polanyi-Levitt, Kari, and Marguerite Mendell. 1987. "Karl Polanyi: His Life and Times." *Studies in Political Economy* 22: 7–39.

References

Polletta, Francesca. 2006. *It Was Like a Fever: Storytelling in Protest and Politics*. Chicago: University of Chicago Press.

Portes, Alejandro. 2010. *Economic Sociology: A Systematic Inquiry*. Princeton, NJ: Princeton University Press.

Powell, Walter W. 1990. "Neither Markets Nor Hierarchy: Network Forms of Organization." *Research in Organizational Behavior* 12: 295–336.

Purser, Gretchen. 2009. "The Dignity of Job-Seeking Men: Boundary Work among Immigrant Day Laborers." *Journal of Contemporary Ethnography* 38(1): 117–39.

Quadagno, Jill. 1994. *The Color of Welfare: How Racism Undermined the War on Poverty*. New York: Oxford University Press.

Quiggin, John. 2010. *Zombie Economics: How Dead Ideas Still Walk among Us*. Princeton, NJ: Princeton University Press.

Raeburn, Nicole C. 2004. *Changing Corporate America from Inside Out: Lesbian and Gay Workplace Rights*. Minneapolis: University of Minnesota Press.

Rao, Hayagreeva. 2009. *Market Rebels: How Activists Make or Break Radical Innovations*. Princeton, NJ: Princeton University Press.

Reich, Robert B. 2010. *Aftershock: The Next Economy and America's Future*. New York: Alfred A. Knopf.

Richards, Lawrence. 2010. *Union-Free America: Workers and Antiunion Culture*. Urbana: University of Illinois Press.

Rivera, Lauren. 2011. "Ivies, Extracurriculars, and Exclusion: Elite Employers' Use of Eductional Credentials." *Research in Social Stratification and Mobility* 29: 71–90.

Rodriguez, Robyn Magalit. 2010. *Migrants for Export: How the Philippine State Brokers Labor to the World*. Minneapolis: University of Minnesota Press.

Roe, Mark J. 1996. *Strong Managers, Weak Owners*. Princeton, NJ: Princeton University Press.

Rosen, Eva, and Sudhir Alladi Venkatesh. 2008. "A 'Perversion' of Choice: Sex Work Offers Just Enough in Chicago's Urban Ghetto." *Journal of Contemporary Ethnography* 37(4): 417–41.

Roth, Louise Marie. 2006. *Selling Women Short: Gender and Money on Wall Street*. Princeton, NJ: Princeton University Press.

Rousseau, Jean-Jacques. 2009 [1762]. *Discourse on Political Economy and The Social Contract*, trans. Christopher Betts. New York: Oxford University Press.

Roy, Donald. 1954. "Efficiency and 'The Fix': Informal Intergroup Relations in a Piecework Machine Shop." *American Journal of Sociology* 60(3): 255–66.

Roy, William G. 1999. *Socializing Capital: The Rise of the Large Industrial Corporation in America*. Princeton, NJ: Princeton University Press.

Sabel, Charles, and Jonathan Zeitlin. 1985. "Historical Alternatives to Mass Production: Politics, Markets and Technology in Nineteenth-Century Industrialization." *Past and Present* 108: 133–76.

References

Sallaz, Jeffrey J. 2002. "The House Rules: Autonomy and Interests among Service Workers in the Contemporary Casino Industry." *Work and Occupations* 29(4): 394–427.

Sallaz, Jeffrey J. 2004. "Manufacturing Concessions: Attritionary Outsourcing at General Motor's Lordstown, USA Assembly Plant." *Work, Employment & Society* 18(4): 687–708.

Sallaz, Jeffrey J. 2009. *The Labor of Luck: Casino Capitalism in the United States and South Africa.* Berkeley: University of California Press.

Sallaz, Jeffrey J. 2010. "Service Work and Symbolic Power: On Putting Bourdieu to Work." *Work and Occupations* 37(3): 295–319.

Sassen, Saskia. 1998. *Globalization and Its Discontents.* New York: New Press.

Schumpeter, Joseph A. 1994 [1942]. *Capitalism, Socialism and Democracy.* New York: Routledge.

Scott, W. Richard, Martin Ruef, Carol A. Caronna, and Peter J. Mendel. 2000. *Institutional Change and Healthcare Organizations: From Professional Dominance to Managed Care.* Chicago: University of Chicago Press.

Seabrooke, Leonard. 2006. *The Social Sources of Financial Power: Domestic Legitimacy and International Financial Orders.* Ithaca, NY: Cornell University Press.

Seidman, Gay W. 1994. *Manufacturing Militance: Workers' Movements in Brazil and South Africa, 1970–1985.* Berkeley: University of California Press.

Seidman, Gay W. 2007. *Beyond the Boycott: Labor Rights, Human Rights, and Transnational Activism.* New York: Russell Sage Foundation.

Sharone, Ofer. 2007. "Constructing Unemployed Job Seekers as Professional Workers: The Depoliticizing Work-Game of Job Searching." *Qualitative Sociology* 30: 403–16.

Sherman, Rachel. 2005. "Producing the Superior Self: Strategic Comparison and Symbolic Boundaries among Luxury Hotel Workers." *Ethnography* 6: 131–58.

Sherman, Rachel. 2007. *Class Acts: Service and Inequality in Luxury Hotels.* Berkeley: University of California Press.

Silver, Beverly J. 2003. *Forces of Labor: Workers' Movements and Globalization since 1870.* New York: Cambridge University Press.

Simmel, Georg. 1950 [1903]. "The Metropolis and Mental Life." In *The Sociology of Georg Simmel*, trans. Kurt Wolff. New York: Free Press, 409–24.

Simmel, Georg. 2011 [1907]. *The Philosophy of Money*, ed. David Frisby. New York: Routledge.

Simon, Herbert A. 1997 [1945]. *Administrative Behavior.* 4th edn. New York: Free Press.

Simon, Herbert A. 1997. *Models of Bounded Rationality, Vol. 3: Empirically Grounded Economic Reason.* Boston, MA: MIT Press.

Skrentny, John David. 1996. *The Ironies of Affirmative Action: Politics, Culture, and Justice in America.* Chicago: University of Chicago Press.

References

Skrentny, John David. 2002. *The Minority Rights Revolution.* Cambridge, MA: Harvard University Press.

Smelser, Neil J. 1959. *Social Change in the Industrial Revolution: An Application of Theory to the British Cotton Industry.* Chicago: University of Chicago Press.

Smith, Adam. 1904 [1776]. *An Inquiry into the Nature and Causes of the Wealth of Nations.* 5th edition. London: Methuen and Co., Ltd.

Smith, Charles W. 1990. *Auctions: The Social Construction of Value.* Berkeley: University of California Press.

Smith, Sandra Susan. 2005. "'Don't Put My Name on It': Social Capital Activation and Job-Finding Assistance among the Black Urban Poor." *American Journal of Sociology* 111(1): 1–57.

Smith, Vicki. 1998. "The Fractured World of the Temporary Worker: Power, Participation, and Fragmentation in the Contemporary Workplace." *Social Problems* 45(4): 411–30.

Smith, Vicki. 2001. *Crossing the Great Divide: Worker Risk and Opportunity in the New Economy.* Ithaca, NY: Cornell University Press.

Smith, Vicki, and Esther B. Neuwirth. 2009. "Temporary Help Agencies and the Making of a New Employment Practice." *Academy of Management Perspectives* 23(1): 56–72.

Solow, Robert M. 1990. *The Labor Market as a Social Institution.* Cambridge, UK: Blackwell.

Spence, Michael. 1973. "Job Market Signaling." *The Quarterly Journal of Economics* 87(3): 355–74.

Stapleford, Thomas A. 2009. *The Cost of Living in America: A Political History of Economic Statistics, 1880–2000.* New York: Cambridge University Press.

Stark, David. 1996. "Recombinant Property in East European Capitalism." *American Journal of Sociology* 101(4): 993–1027.

Steensland, Brian. 2007. *The Failed Welfare Revolution: America's Struggle over Guaranteed Income Policy.* Princeton, NJ: Princeton University Press.

Steiner, Philippe. 2010. *Durkheim and the Birth of Economic Sociology,* trans. Keith Tribe. Princeton, NJ: Princeton University Press.

Stinchcombe, Arthur L. 1959. "Bureaucratic and Craft Administration of Production: A Comparative Study." *Administrative Science Quarterly* 4(2): 168–87.

Storper, Michael, and Robert Salais. 1997. *Worlds of Production: The Action Frameworks of the Economy.* Cambridge, MA: Harvard University Press.

Strange, Susan. 1996. *The Retreat of the State: The Diffusion of Power in the World Economy.* New York: Cambridge University Press.

Stryker, Robin. 2001. "Disparate Impact and the Quota Debates: Law, Labor Market Sociology, and Equal Employment Policies." *The Sociological Quarterly* 42(1): 13–46.

Sutton, John R., Frank Dobbin, John W. Meyer, and W. Richard Scott. 1994.

References

"The Legalization of the Workplace." *American Journal of Sociology* 99(4): 944–71.

Swartz, David. 1998. *Culture and Power: The Sociology of Pierre Bourdieu.* Chicago: University of Chicago Press.

Swedberg, Richard. 2000. *Max Weber and the Idea of Economic Sociology.* Princeton, NJ: Princeton University Press.

Swidler, Ann. 1986. "Culture in Action: Symbols and Strategies." *American Sociological Review* 51(2): 273–86.

Tabuchi, Hiroko. 2009. "Japan Pays Foreign Workers to Go Home." *The New York Times*, April 23, sec. Business/Global Business. http://www.nytimes.com/2009/04/23/business/global/23immigrant.html (accessed July 31, 2012).

Taylor, Frederick Winslow. 1913. *The Principles of Scientific Management.* New York: Harper & Brothers Publishing.

Telles, Edward E. 2004. *Race in Another America: The Significance of Skin Color in Brazil.* Princeton, NJ: Princeton University Press.

Thelen, Kathleen. 2004. *How Institutions Evolve: The Political Economy of Skills in Germany, Britain, the United States, and Japan.* New York: Cambridge University Press.

Thompson, E. P. 1966. *The Making of the English Working Class.* New York: Vintage.

Thoreau, Henry David. 1854. *Walden, or, Life in the Woods.* Boston, MA: Ticknor and Fields.

Tilly, Charles. 1985. "War Making and State Making as Organized Crime." In *Bringing the State Back In*, ed. Peter B. Evans, Dietrich Rueschemeyer, and Theda Skocpol. New York: Cambridge University Press, 169–91.

Tilly, Charles. 1999. *Durable Inequality.* Berkeley: University of California Press.

Tilly, Chris, and Charles Tilly. 1997. *Work under Capitalism.* Boulder, CO: Westview Press.

Useem, Michael. 1999. *Investor Capitalism: How Money Managers are Changing the Face of Corporate America.* New York: Basic Books.

Uzzi, Brian. 1997. "Social Structure and Competition in Interfirm Networks: The Paradox of Embeddedness." *Administrative Science Quarterly* 42(1): 35–67.

Voss, Kim, and Rachel Sherman. 2000. "Breaking the Iron Law of Oligarchy: Union Revitalization in the American Labor Movement." *American Journal of Sociology* 106(2): 303–49.

Wacquant, Loïc, ed. 2005. *Pierre Bourdieu and Democratic Politics: The Mystery of Ministry.* Cambridge, MA: Polity.

Waldinger, Roger, and Michael I. Lichter. 2003. *How the Other Half Works: Immigration and the Social Organization of Labor.* Berkeley: University of California Press.

Wallerstein, Immanuel. 2011. *The Modern World-System IV: Centrist Liberalism Triumphant, 1789–1914.* Berkeley: University of California Press.

References

Wathne, Kenneth H., and Jan B. Heide. 2004. "Relationship Governance in a Supply Chain Network." *The Journal of Marketing* 68(1): 73–89.

Weber, Max. 1978 [1922]. *Economy and Society: An Outline of Interpretive Sociology.* Berkeley: University of California Press.

Weber, Max. 2003 [1930]. *The Protestant Ethic and the Spirit of Capitalism*, trans. Talcott Parsons. Mineola, NY: Courier Dover Publications.

Western, Bruce. 1999. *Between Class and Market: Postwar Unionization in the Capitalist Democracies.* Princeton, NJ: Princeton University Press.

Western, Bruce. 2007. *Punishment and Inequality in America.* New York: Russell Sage Foundation.

Whitford, Josh, and Cuz Potter. 2007. "Regional Economies, Open Networks and the Spatial Fragmentation of Production." *Socio-Economic Review* 5(3): 497–526.

Whyte, William Foote. 1948. *Human Relations in the Restaurant Industry.* New York: McGraw Hill.

Williams, Christine L., and Catherine Connell. 2010. "'Looking Good and Sounding Right': Aesthetic Labor and Social Inequality in the Retail Industry." *Work and Occupations* 37(3): 349–77.

Williamson, Oliver E. 1998. *The Economic Institutions of Capitalism.* New York: Free Press.

Willis, Paul. 1981. *Learning to Labor: How Working Class Kids Get Working Class Jobs.* New York: Columbia University Press.

Wright, Erik Olin. 2000. "Working-Class Power, Capitalist-Class Interests, and Class Compromise." *American Journal of Sociology* 105(4): 957–1002.

Yakubovich, Valery, Mark Granovetter, and Patrick Mcguire. 2005. "Electric Charges: The Social Construction of Rate Systems." *Theory and Society* 34: 579–612.

Zelizer, Viviana A. 1981. "The Price and Value of Children: The Case of Children's Insurance." *American Journal of Sociology* 86: 1036–56.

Zelizer, Viviana A. 1997. *The Social Meaning of Money: Pin Money, Paychecks, Poor Relief, and Other Currencies.* Princeton, NJ: Princeton University Press.

Index

Page numbers in **bold type** refer to a figure.

Index

Index

Index

Index